TRILOGY #2

CONTENTS

ABOUT THE AUTHOR

Born in the depression year of 1930, the eighth of nine children, Linden's parents never fully recovered from those hard times which began to get better in 1941. Starting at age 13, his work life included labor on a dairy farm, grocery store clerk, night janitor during his last two years of high school, flooring tile cutter, construction, truck driver, and collector-salesman before entering the Air Force at age 21. At this time, he had been married two years.

The worst part of his four-year Air Force stint was the ending of his first marriage and the best part probably was playing on a good basketball team while stationed in California. After discharge, he joined the Indiana State Police in April of 1956 as a Morse code operator and later was instrumental in developing the Indiana computerized law enforcement information system and writing the first operations manual for that system.

Linden left the State Police in 1977 to begin working for the Department of Welfare and later the Department of Correction in the data processing and communications areas. After retiring from State government duties in 1996, he did a bit of consulting work and served as a credit union Director and as Chairman of an Indiana E-911 committee. He also worked part time in real estate sales during his time with the State.

He remarried in 1962 and was blessed with a son, Brian, in 1963, and a daughter, Julie, in 1966. This marriage ended in 1984. After a few difficult years, he was blessed with the companionship of a wonderful woman, Rubye Creech. She passed away in 2003. He continues to live alone in Plainfield, Indiana and is visited frequently by his two wonderful children and less often by any of his six grandchildren. Linden has been an active member of Plainfield, Indiana Christian Church for over forty years.

In 1983, after wondering about how he would spend his time after retiring, Linden wrote his first book. He also wrote a few songs that became a CD featuring Peter Smith on the guitar and Linden singing…Peter and Rubye's daughter, Lisa Smith, join in the singing of one of the songs. In recent years, Linden offered many mostly politically oriented blog postings at www.linden-would.blogspot.com .

This book is a compilation of three of Linden's books that were previously published. Hopefully you and others will benefit from   reading his writings.

A SWIFT:
NOT JONATHAN

Copyright © 2008 by Linden H. Swift

Consulting Editor   Sharon Herbitter

Printed by Augustin Printers, Richmond, IN

LINDENWOULD PUBLISHING CO. INC.

BOX 203 PLAINFIELD   IN 46168-0203

CONTENTS

FOREWORD

I would not be surprised if this, my seventh self-published book, is the last of those published under the Lindenwould imprint. Writing can be quite enjoyable but sales efforts are work and I'm getting too old for the pitiful efforts I make in that regard.

My Consulting Editor, Sharon Herbitter, has been an inspiration to me and her writing ability far exceeds that of mine. Her Internet Commentary praise of this compilation and of the CD I produced a short time ago was heartwarming. I am blest in so many ways.

Only Sharon has seen this entire collection but I have very pleasant memories of sharing some of it with my dear departed Rubye and, to a lesser degree, some with my children, Brian and Julie.

My sister, Edna, gave me the two In Memoriam poems contained herein shortly before her death. I love them. I believe they have not been seen before.

If you should be interested in my other works, purchasing information is often included in my Internet musings at www.linden-would.blogspot.com

Linden Swift, October 2008

The back cover of the print edition of this work contained the following words written by Sharon Herbitter.

"Linden Swift has gathered together in this short book a little something for everybody: from a frog pond to Judgment Day, songs to short stories, themes to make you laugh and some that will make you cry.

Linden's first CD was released just a few months back and he includes the lyrics to those songs as well as notes that describe how each song was created. The short stories—some frightening, some amusing, all entertaining—are bite-sized yet satisfying portions. The play, "Judgment Day," gives insight into his personal faith.

It is Linden's poetry, however, that shines the brightest. He has an ear for rhyme and rhythm in written form and expresses his emotions simply and clearly in a profound and moving way. As an additional treat, he has included two excellent poems written by his late sister, Edna Swift Northerner. Poetry must be a heritable trait."

STORIES

A MODEST PROPOSAL (2006)

I sometimes use the word "modest" in conjunction with my needs, wants, income and net worth, but rarely use it when writing. I cheerfully admit that the title of this piece was shamelessly stolen from the 1729 writings of Jonathan Swift, now best known as the author of *Gulliver's Travels*.

His "Modest Proposal" was "For Preventing the Children of Poor People in Ireland from Being a Burden to Their Parents or Country, and for Making Them Beneficial to the Publick." My proposal, although potentially beneficial, will be much less ambitious than his.

Those of us who are interested in the political process are in general agreement that all efforts to control political campaign fundraising and spending have been miserable failures. My proposal, if adopted, will return a modicum of sanity and decency to this problem area.

First, all fundraising must be conducted solely by the candidate and must be conducted within the confines of the area to be represented. Since many officeholders, particularly senators, are really citizens of the Washington, D.C. area and are citizens of the states they represent only by the wildest stretch of the imagination, this constraint will require them to become reacquainted with those they represent.

Second, donors may contribute only their own personal funds. This should effectively close most PACs.

Third, donors must place contributions, one dollar at a time, in the tin cup, bucket, barrel or other receptacle used by the candidate. The candidate must shake the hand of the donor and say "thank you" after each one-dollar contribution. Estimates set the maximum donated amount in any 12-hour period to be $43,200.

Fourth, gifts of transportation, housing, event tickets and food with a value of over $50 in any one month are not permitted. This further reduces the influence of special interests. Benefit to the taxpayer is increased time the officeholder may devote to service. Benefit to the officeholder is additional time for fundraising efforts.

Fifth, officeholders who earmark funds for pet projects or fail to oppose a personally beneficial pay raise will not be eligible to hold any office for four years following the end of their current term. This single item will result in the saving of billions of taxpayer dollars.

Sixth, unspent campaign funds following the affected general election will be used to reduce the federal deficit.

Seventh, an auditing office will process all donated funds and distribute them as follows: 10 percent each to the appropriate national and state committees and 20 percent to the appropriate county committee. If more than one county is involved, distribution within the area will be based on population. The candidate may use the remaining 60 percent.

Penalties for failing to adhere to the direction or intent of this proposal will result in heavy fines and permanent ineligibility to hold elective office.

Independent analysts predict that adoption of this proposal will result in there being no further need for term-limit legislation.

THE INSIDERLUNGS (2006)

"Daddy," the curly-haired little girl said as she interrupted her father's reading of the daily paper. "Tell me what makes a brain work."

"Well," said Daddy as he laid his paper aside. "Just climb up on my lap and you will soon know more on that subject than anyone else in the first grade." The little girl settled on his lap and the story began.

"You remember the old German story I told you of the Nibelungs, the little dwarf people who lived underground? Well, I've never told you about the Insiderlungs, the even smaller creatures that live inside your body. I guess it's time you heard that story.

"They are very, very tiny and have as many as six arms, although they move so fast that no scientist has ever seen more than two arms. They are so tiny that very few have ever been seen—they are most often referred to as 'brain cells' or 'synapses.' They have the job of passing information within the brain. They accomplish this by passing notes to each other.

"These notes usually end up being something you say or do. Sometimes a fun-loving Insiderlung will replace the note he has been passed with one from the note bin— this often results in the wrong thing being said or done.

Wrong answers on tests and people saying swear words are two examples of an Insiderlung acting bad.

"Insiderlungs are happiest when they are working at passing information notes and they often become upset when people go to bed. When nighttime comes, an Insiderlung passes a note saying 'time for bed,' 'stretch,' 'wiggle your toes,' 'close your eyes' and 'breathe deeply.' Soon you are asleep. The note passing then gradually slows down until it stops. Then, an unruly Insiderlung may start passing notes that result in you having a dream, or, if it's a bad-tempered Insiderlung, even a very bad dream called a nightmare.

"When there are no notes that cause dreams to be passed, the note passing stops entirely and the Insiderlungs start to grumble and complain because there is no work to do. They have their own language that no human can understand, but in their language they are saying, 'No, no work to do, no notes to pass'— so many of them are complaining that they can be heard. Usually the sleeper is breathing deeply with his mouth wide open; most humans call the sound of the complaining Insiderlungs 'snoring.'"

As Daddy ended the story, he looked down at the little girl and said, "Well, it looks like my little princess has gone to sleep and I can already hear the Insiderlungs starting to complain."

WHERE IS SAFETY? (2006)

At 10:00 A.M. on Wednesday, April 30, 1975, the man who was to become my friend some fifteen years later and half a world away, left his home in South Vietnam. He was not to return for at least the years between then and now and, as this is written, perhaps never again. He, a government official, now that his government was in the process of falling to the communist government of North Vietnam, was in danger of losing his life in an unpleasant way.

At 4:00 P.M. he again approached the home he shared with his wife and young son. It was a three-story house with offices on the first floor and living quarters above. He was accompanied by two friends, each a high ranking police or army officer. All three were acutely aware of the mortal danger they were in and they, fearing a trap, decided not to enter his home. Instead, they struck out down the adjacent river in a police boat which they had commandeered. Each one carried a grenade and a cyanide tablet in case suicide became the best option. It was a time and a place where misplacing your trust could easily cost you your life.

There were many boats on the river; they were peopled by turncoats, spies, and those fleeing for their lives to destinations yet to be determined. Those on the boat which the friends had commandeered had neither food nor water for the first two days of their journey. By this time, they had reached the ocean. Shortly thereafter they were able to join 32 others on a larger boat; at this time they were given a small amount of food and water.

This larger boat had originally started with provisions for 23 people and now had 35 aboard. This, of course, caused a great deal of concern about being adequately provisioned. There were a great deal of secret conversations among the original members and the three we are most concerned with took turns sleeping, as they feared that they might be killed if they failed to remain alert. They always had their grenades and cyanide tablets readily available.

It was on this boat where my friend heard that a friend of his had mentioned him in a radio broadcast. The friend had offered relative, and perhaps temporary, safety in an adjacent province. This was reported to my friend by those in another boat which contained about a hundred persons, many of them friends and former classmates of my friend.

They entered into a discussion concerning the possibility of the broadcast being the result of the broadcaster being in enemy hands and being forced to make the announcement. Eventually, the three friends decided to remain on the boat they were on and take their chances on the high seas. Those on the other boat chose to make the attempt to reach the other province. Their boat struck a mine and blew up. There were probably few, if any, survivors.

During all this time, the three friends remained aware of possible attack by others on the boat. They were fully prepared to commit suicide if that became the most desirable course of action. They participated in protecting the boat they were on when they were attacked by those on other boats who needed to increase their supply of gasoline, food and water. It seemed that every boat was well supplied with military weapons which the crew members were more than willing to use in the hope that it would increase their chances of staying alive.

The boat containing the three friends continued out into the ocean where, on about the fifth day, a large ship circled their boat. Although the little boat flashed the appropriate distress signals, it was to no avail; the large ship sailed away. The next day, the little boat encountered three Taiwanese fishing boats. At first they would not take the passengers on the little boat on board but, when learning that my friend and two others were known in Taiwan, did allow them aboard and fed them very little until their bodies recovered. About fourteen days after it started, the first part of their ordeal was effectively over.

Several months later, my friend was trying to find a meaningful life in the United States. Some eight years later, my friend was joined by his wife and their son and was on his way to a productive life in his new country.

The title of this writing, "Where Is Safety?" was selected to cause you to consider where you would attempt to go if our country should fall. Perhaps there is no other place.

THE GIVER/TAKER WORLD (2006)

"Dad, why is it," asked twelve-year-old Billy Ferrell as the two of them returned from a pleasant outing, "that most of my friends have Dads who work regular jobs, are usually short of money and their lives seem much more difficult than ours?"

"Well," replied Brian Ferrell, "as you may come to understand tomorrow, it is a giver/taker world and all I do is take advantage of opportunities that present themselves. According to your birth certificate, you will be thirteen years old at exactly 11:26 A.M. tomorrow and that is when we will find out if you have the gift. I expect, since it is deeply ingrained in our ancestry, that you will."

Shortly after 11:00 the next day, Billy and his Dad were in a restaurant in downtown Chicago. Billy was dressed in clean, neat and slightly worn clothing while Brian had on an obviously expensive suit. "Son," said Brian, "I'll order a cup of coffee and I want you to walk around the block, not too fast, and look for opportunities. We'll have lunch when you return."

Billy had not walked far and the time must have been 11:26 because he saw a well-dressed man approaching. The man had a luminous sign on his forehead which blinked on and off. The sign said "GIVER."

"Pardon me sir," said Billy. "I wonder if you could give me some advice. My mom is very sick, we are out of groceries and Dad has abandoned us—I wonder if you could tell me how I may earn some money—I have to take care of my Mom."

"No," said the man. "I'm late for a meeting so there is no time to talk. But," as he reached for his wallet, "here is something that will help." He handed Billy a crisp twenty-dollar bill.

"Thank you and God bless you, sir," said Billy and walked on.

It was amazing—some people had no apparent sign on their foreheads, some had, in various shades, yellow signs which said "TAKER"—no point in talking to them—and several had those luminous red "GIVER" signs which blinked on and off. Billy was later to learn that the intensity of the color and the rapidity of the blinking were accurate indicators of a person's readiness to give. He also learned that he was marked with the yellow sign.

Before Brian's coffee had time to cool, Billy was back and placed fifty-two dollars on the table in front of his dad. "I'm proud of you, son—let's order our lunch. I want you to watch me this afternoon as I conduct a seminar on how to become a millionaire by buying investment property. Maybe tomorrow our whole family will go to Las Vegas for a celebration."

It seemed that all was right and good.

ANOTHER MODEST PROPOSAL (2006)

It seems most citizens agree that our legislative bodies, particularly at the federal level, are composed of those who are much more concerned with personal enrichment or continuing their "service" than they are in actually serving the citizenry. For some unexplainable reason, these same citizens do not see the one representing their own particular district as being part of the overall problem. This has led to a very high rate of incumbent retention and, concurrently, usually much fatter campaign treasuries for the incumbent.

It also seems that practically every state in our nation has become addicted to gambling as a means of fattening the state treasuries. The initial approach is often sold as a means of providing funds for what is presented as a much-needed enterprise, such as education. Many believe state-sponsored gambling has not been the blessing it was predicted to be.

This proposal suggests that since state-sponsored gambling is not likely to be repealed, opposition candidate selection and initial funding should be accomplished by means of lottery ticket sales. Top prize would be an amount equal to the pay for one year for the office being sought plus instant name recognition within the affected district. A convicted felon would not be eligible for candidacy but, if one holds the winning ticket, would receive an amount equal to 10 percent of the aforementioned prize. It is left to the enacting bodies to more fully develop this proposal.

LARRY AND HORACE (2007)

Larry, the poisonous spider, was not a real bad guy. Oh sure, some of the small bugs and even some other spiders that he used for a food supply would not agree—but one does have to eat. Right? Even those who constituted his food supply would agree that, always considerate, he would spray them with a numbing agent before moving in for the kill. In fact, Larry had no real dislike for any living creature . . . except for Horace! Larry's fondest dream was to KILL Horace!

On the other hand, Horace didn't really like anybody or anything. He lived alone in his small apartment, going out for little other than groceries. He was a meticulous housekeeper who occupied his time dusting, vacuuming, watching television and sometimes writing a little. He had absolutely no idea that Larry even existed, let alone the possibility that Larry had seen him run the vacuum over the love of Larry's life, Emily.

One day, as was not uncommon in the quiet of the very early morning hours, Larry was moving slowly across the bathroom wall thinking of his next meal. Suddenly the light came on and a very sleepy Horace entered. Soon, he noticed Larry, motionless on the wall. Not hesitating, Horace folded two sheets of tissue together and a short time later Larry had been captured and thrown into the commode.

Disoriented and slightly injured from the capture, Larry struggled to regain his senses after being dropped into the cold water. It seemed like only seconds later there was a sound and the water started swirling down with Larry trying to grab on to any small protrusion in the plumbing. Finally, after what seemed like an eternity, Larry attached himself to a small plumbing imperfection and held on for dear life. When the flushing action stopped, Larry found himself in an air pocket and was, for the moment, safe—although certainly feeling rather badly used.

Some time later, Larry heard the rushing water coming again; he flattened himself against his protective niche and determined to try to escape. It was anything but easy but he did make his way through the water until he arrived at the basin where he had originally been thrown. He made his way up the side of the basin and hid under the rim for three days, venturing out only at night and only to find food. At the end of this three-day period his strength had returned and he was ready to go hunting for big game.

The next time Horace sat on the commode while reading the morning paper Larry carefully made his way from his hiding place under the commode rim to the exposed skin of Horace. He sprayed a small amount of the numbing agent on the skin before becoming an unknown passenger on Horace's body. Sometimes

Larry would spend extended periods of time within a body orifice, other times on the skin and sometimes at night he would venture away from the body in order to hunt his food.

On the first day of residing on and in Horace, Larry started injecting small amounts of poison into his system. After some weeks of this, Horace had seen his doctor twice in an unsuccessful effort to determine why he seemed to be feeling so much worse than was normal. Horace no longer felt well enough to do the usual house cleaning and he spent more and more time being in a half-awake condition on his bed. Larry used these times to increase the number of injections.

Late one evening, while Horace was motionless on his bed, Larry made a large injection of poison directly into the large vein that was in the crease of Horace's thigh. Horace twitched three times and Larry could feel the body shutting down. Larry made his way back into the body orifice, intending to have an extended rest period. The next day he felt cold, so he remained inactive. Much later, after feeling the body being moved several times, Larry felt it getting warmer, much warmer. Then Larry was gone.

Now, Larry and Horace are together forever—in the ashes within a crematory urn.

SECRETS, ILLEGALS AND MATTER TRANSMISSION (2007)

Return with me for a moment, if you will, to a time in our history when those of the ilk of Sandy Berger faced swift, certain and appropriate punishment. A time when the "Justice Department" was not a laughingstock and many of those in congress appeared to be more interested in the welfare of our country than they were in their own reelection. It was a long time ago.

It is almost impossible to imagine a time when security was so efficiently managed that even The New York Times either did not publish a leak or, more likely, was not aware of the affected secret. I am speaking of the massive secret effort which resulted in the atomic bomb being dropped on Japan—thereby shortening the war and saving many lives.

I envision such a current secret effort and expect it, when fully developed, to be utilized in a manner to be outlined later. You are aware, no doubt, that illegal aliens are and have been flooding into our country and that congress has addressed this problem with its usual ineptitude. You may also be aware that many writings have been posted and that a patent has been applied for in the field of matter transmission.

Now, let us imagine the development of this matter transmission capability and its utilization by the governmental department, if any, which is responsible for controlling immigration. When operational, it will consist of a shielded, scannable room that is large enough to hold several large objects or people.

In operation, this matter transmission equipment will be much like a photocopier, x-ray machine or MRI device. It will have a numbering system to facilitate reconstruction of that which is being transmitted. Operating indicators will include "Send," "Receive," "Reconstituted in New Location?" and "Retransmit."

Imagine a family being placed in this deportation room, the "Send" button being depressed, scanning occurring and, for a small fraction of a second, the family is existent in two places: the sending location and the receiving location. If the family is properly reconstructed in its new location, the sending location is notified and the family disappears from the deportation room and is immediately functional in its new location.

As an example, a family of five is placed in the deportation room and relocated to, perhaps, Mexico City. They are reconstructed in the receiving room that is located on a truck which is parked on a quiet street. The entire process is completed in less than five minutes. All documents accompanying the family, including a small amount of relocation money, is reconstructed also. Their belongings left behind are liquidated. If the children were born here, they will have to prove citizenship if and when they ever return.

When fully operational, with one machine operating continuously in each of the fifty states, more than five million deportations are possible per year. With lack of secrecy and theft being ever-present possibilities, we should expect this capability to soon be available in the private sector on a limited basis. This could result in a small group of government "leaders" being kidnapped and being quickly reconstituted on a street corner in, perhaps, Baghdad. If that time should come, I have some names to submit for consideration.

THE TRAPPER

("Just the paper please," said Ted Blake as he took a fifty-dollar bill from the large roll in his front pocket and laid it on the convenience store counter.

"That the least you got?" said the rather sullen young man behind the counter.

"Yeah, lucky me."

The exact same scene had been replayed several times in the ten days Ted had lived in this rather depressed multicultural area. It was the third such city and area he had lived in since retiring from a large metropolitan police department.

Upon arriving in a new city, Ted always visited the police department and police support groups and searched for opportunities to meet those officers who served in the area within which he lived. He made a good impression and was so easy to talk to that he often joined a group of officers as they had their meals and coffee breaks.

As Ted walked across the convenience store parking lot and down the alley that led to the steps to his second floor apartment, he passed the garage where he and a downstairs neighbor could keep their cars. The downstairs apartment was now vacant. The garage door was offset about three feet back of the connected concrete block storage building, which the tenants could also share.

Ted climbed up the fifteen steps to the small deck that led to the door of the porch from which entry to the apartment was made. Strong pillars supported the porch and in the space below was the entrance to the basement laundry room. The porch had screened windows on every side with glass window frames which could be hooked to the ceiling to permit airflow.

The door opening to the apartment from the porch revealed a small kitchen with a small bathroom immediately to the left of the entrance. Straight through was an opening which led to the combination living-dining room: Ted had installed a beaded curtain on this doorway. Beyond this room were the bedroom and closet areas. Ted was elated that, in this area, he was able to find a furnished apartment which so completely met his needs and wants.

Ted had installed security cameras which provided a view of the area in front of the storage area and garage, the stairs leading up to the apartment and the entry to the back porch. Ted could monitor any activity in these areas from either the living room or his bedroom. A low sound alerted him when a motion sensor detected any activity. He felt very secure even though the neighborhood did not warrant such a feeling.

It was just after 2:00 a.m. when the motion detector alerted Ted to outside activity. He checked the security camera picture images and, sure enough, the car used by the local gang of toughs was idling with its lights off in the parking area in front of the storage building. The car had a very distinctive sound but Ted, while watching television, had not heard the car. This particular gang of young toughs, which included the convenience store clerk, had often been the topic of conversation when Ted had visited with his local law enforcement friends.

Ted went to the kitchen, flipped on the light switch and then on to the bathroom where he turned on the light, the shower and a cassette recording of him singing. He then crawled out of the bathroom so he wouldn't be visible from the outside. Then closed the bathroom door and crawled to the living room area. As he crept through the kitchen he noted that it sounded like he was enjoying a shower in the bathroom.

Ted then started monitoring the security camera images. After a time, three figures quietly exited the car, climbed the steps and hesitated outside the bathroom window to hear the sounds of showering inside. One of the gang of three had a gun, another a shortened baseball bat and the third a switchblade knife. The one with the knife cut the screen, reached inside and turned the knob. They were then inside and only a second later had silently entered the kitchen and were listening, they thought, to Ted showering. The thug with the bat was closest to the bathroom; next, the one with the knife; and the one with the gun was beside the kitchen entry door.

After the three had whispered their plan, the one next to the bathroom door reached for the doorknob. Immediately Ted, who was hidden behind the beaded curtain with only a bit of the nose of his pistol protruding through, fired twice and the thug with the gun and the one with the knife fell to the floor, twitching in their death throes. Terrified, the third thug turned toward the curtain only to be met with the slug which ended his life "Guess all that time I spent on the firing range really paid off," thought Ted as he heard the car below speed off.

Since it was obviously a home invasion case and since, as a police department retiree Ted was permitted to have a weapon for personal protection, the investigation was quickly over. The removal of the bodies took only slightly longer and before daylight Ted was ready for a long nap. Having just tied his best trapping record, he drifted off in a happy frame of mind.

After awakening, Ted soon made his way to the convenience store where he paid the even more sullen clerk with exact change for the paper. They exchanged no conversation. Later in the day Ted had several opportunities to visit with some of his buddies who were on the local police force. Needless to say, he was viewed as the hero of the day. On several occasions he said, "This area may be too dangerous for me to consider it as a permanent retirement home."

At dusk the next evening, while walking toward his garage, Ted heard the sound of the gang's car approaching at a high rate of speed. He jumped into the garage offset while concurrently drawing his pistol. The right front fender of the car grazed the storage building wall area that he had just vacated and went careening across the convenience store parking lot. Ted got off two quick shots that hit the gas tank which exploded and enveloped the car in flames as it hit a telephone pole. The four occupants never knew what happened.

"Well, nuts!" said Ted to himself. "This may have set a new trapping record but it surely will delay my trip to Cleveland."

On the next day there was a "HELP WANTED" sign on the convenience store door.

THE ULTIMATE PONZI SCHEME (2005)

A Ponzi scheme is a scam whereby some "investors" show a net profit, some break even and the vast majority lose every dime of their so-called investment. This scheme takes its name from 1920s-era Charles Ponzi; you may be interested in researching his <u>illegal</u> actions. Naturally, the ultimate scheme of this type would be one which is not only legal but one within which participation is required. Think "Federal Old Age Benefits" (Social Security). In a nutshell, this program requires about 15 percent of wages (half by the employee and half as a benefit paid by the employer) be contributed for the benefit of existing beneficiaries.

I truly appreciate, not that they have any choice, my two wonderful children funding this portion of my retirement income. In my work life, I was totally unaware that I was funding the retirement of my dad and various unknown persons.

In an earlier time, I trusted the program—or, more likely, never thoroughly analyzed it from a cost/benefit standpoint. When analyzed, one does not have to be a math major to detect glaring shortcomings. I have heard and believe the number of payers to the system in relation to those receiving benefits has been trending downward for many years.

What cash benefits accrue to the estate of those who die before reaching retirement age? Answer: essentially none! A recent local newspaper listing the deaths within the area showed 22 persons from age 20 through age 64. Their estates were victims of The Ultimate Ponzi Scheme. If a reasonable portion of their contributions had been diverted to a personal account and if both their income and account interest earned were quite modest, surely those personal accounts would have been valued at more than $1,000 and possibly, for the older ones, more than $100,000.

Please do not misunderstand me: by living well beyond the monthly payment start date, my personal objections are few, if any. But, why any reasonably intelligent younger person, member of Congress or organization of senior citizens would be opposed to changing this broken system completely escapes this writer.

SPITTERS—A PRELIMINARY STUDY (2007)

The very title of this piece strongly suggests that it is not a completed work, but perhaps one that does warrant further study. It compares to Kittyhawk versus transatlantic flights or, possibly, learning the alphabet versus writing War and Peace. In other words, there is work yet to be done.

Baseball aficionados may well expect to be exposed to a learned, although preliminary, study of the effect of applying saliva to a baseball before it is delivered up to a bewildered batter. But no, this is not to be. It is rather a study of grown men expectorating, willy-nilly, in the general area of a baseball diamond.

Since major league baseball outlawed, with some exceptions, spitball pitching about ten years before I was born, I suppose I could have written something such as, "Burleigh Grimes may well have been the last of the great spitball pitchers." This would have led to a certain segment of society considering me to be a great historian. I have no need of such cheap and meaningless accolades. You may consider me to be only a dedicated research scientist.

There are now thirty major league teams with an average of about twenty-eight players and five on the bench or field management personnel. A thorough study of this type would require that each of these almost one thousand persons be monitored for every inning of every game and the number of spits per person per game be carefully recorded. With my present life expectancy being somewhat less than nine years, you can readily see that I had time for only a preliminary study.

My approach was to watch televised game-spitting activity, a relatively low number of games and only three innings of each game. Anything longer than three innings and I would lose my ability to concentrate. I could hardly believe that, using these restrictive guidelines, I once saw a manager spit five times faster than I could count to five. I mathematically extended the data collected to represent what could have been the total if the data had been collected in an optimum manner.

As we view my findings, please remember the aforementioned data collection limitations and apply them to the findings. It appears there were 9.6 spits per participant, per game. This becomes 316.8 spits per team, per game, 51,321.6 spits per team, per season and a major league total of 1,539,648 spits per season.

There are an estimated 36 spits per liquid ounce or 4,608 spits per gallon. This comes to only a little over 334 gallons per season: I anticipated a higher number. Surely I made no computational errors.

As a side note, what I watched of the All-Star Game indicated that the National League spits about forty percent more than the American League. Also, in my limited viewing it appeared that the Chicago White Sox were the spittingest team.

I intended to compute how wet a season's total spit would make the line from home plate to first base but I'm . . . I'm . . . getting . . . sleepy . . .

BUSY HANDS ARE HAPPY HANDS (2004)

The title of this piece is not original—it was dredged from my forty-year-old memories of a coworker's favorite sayings. Nor, as you undoubtedly know, is it always true. We are sometimes engaged in activity that is anything but happy, and in times of great personal grief we must refocus our thinking before happiness can come again. However, regardless of our age, keeping busy is a good recipe for moving toward a more happy state of mind.

As I approached the "golden years," my thoughts often turned to the subject of what my interests should be when I was no longer gainfully employed. Fortunately, I was already somewhat politically active and was involved with various church-related activities. Well before calling it quits in the work force, I decided to turn to writing and publishing as further means of keeping myself occupied when workplace concerns lessened. It is now eight years since my second full-time employment retirement. The three aforementioned activities can be undertaken by anyone at any age.

I do not remember when I first became extremely interested in the political process. This interest may very well have been cemented by reading a short piece entitled "Why I Am a Republican." My first direct political responsibility came about twenty-five years ago when I was appointed Precinct Committeeman—a position which primarily entails representing the Party interest within a geographic area. Either through election or appointment I functioned in this position for over twenty years.

About twenty years ago, at the urging of my high-school-aged daughter (who served as my Vice Committeeman), I became actively involved in the campaigns of another person; this continued through five successful campaigns. She and her husband remain treasured friends. I have been involved with the campaigns of others and, on my own behalf have been elected to serve as a Delegate to our State Convention eleven times, served one term on our County Council and, later, ran unsuccessfully for the same position. Numerous other involvements will not be addressed now. For you to participate in this area of service, simply call someone you know to be involved and ask for advice.

My father was the greatest influence on my early journey of faith. I was baptized in a country church ceremony at the age of eleven. After years of having my adherence to faith wax and wane, I started, when my children were small, to take much more seriously my relationship with the Lord. My faith continues to grow stronger year by year. I currently serve as an active member of the Benevolence Committee within my church. For you to become involved in this activity, I recommend you visit Bible-believing churches until you find the one where you feel comfortable, then contact the church office and offer to help in any way you can. This could easily be the most important thing you will ever do.

Something over twenty years ago, I, as previously mentioned, started writing for publication. Not having much faith in the workings of the submission process, I formed my own company for the purpose of publishing some of my writings. To date I have published five books and have others planned. Sales are never large and are accomplished mostly by word-of-mouth advertising. Most years the company shows a modest profit. You could start in this area by keeping a daily journal or by writing out your prayers.

I hope this writing will be thought provoking for you.

ESTATE PLANNING (2006)

"My richest gain I count but loss, and pour contempt on all my pride." . . . Isaac Watts, 1674-1748

I make this report in order for the executors of my will to know that I have left no stone unturned to rectify the effects of my dissolute youth, careless middle age and haphazard entry into the "golden years." Rest assured, I would now prefer that I had taken a more disciplined approach to living life and thereby, perhaps, relieved those who could have benefited financially upon my passing from some of the pain the vagaries of life bring to the majority of us.

Although many would consider a yard sale to be an inconsequential event, in my life this is not true at all. Please refer to the first sentence in the paragraph above. Even though a sale of this type will represent a miniscule return on the original cost of the items sold, it will be better than nothing. It is my hope that the accounting of items sold will, somehow, show my concern for my loved ones. Invest wisely, dear children.

LETTER TO LAURA (2005)

(Never Mailed)

Dear Laura,

I feel certain you will overlook or at least forgive errors of any kind or type that may be contained herein. This, of course, includes the lack of formality in the greeting.

I have memories of every First Lady since the time of Eleanor Roosevelt and I believe you have established the bar by which they, their predecessors and all future persons in that position should be compared.

I have twice, at inauguration time, intended to send a note to your husband but, not surprisingly, never followed through. My wonderful (now deceased) lady friend, Rubye and I watched the inauguration of 2001 while we were traveling in the Brownsville, Texas area. The content of that never-mailed note to your husband is as follows:

> "As a 71-year-old weeper, my eyes were not dry on your inauguration day from the opening prayer delivered by Franklin Graham until after your fine speech. As a Republican activist who contributed modestly to your election effort, who has met each of your parents and hopes to meet you sometime, I

want you to know that I expect a great deal of you. I'm pleased with what I've seen to date.

I recognize that you will probably not personally see this note, but, perhaps, the gist of it will be conveyed to you. May God's blessing be granted to you and yours and may you succeed in your efforts on behalf of our country."

I believe history will list your husband as one of the greatest of those who have held the office of President. Rest assured, if there is the same type of list for that of First Lady, your name will prominently appear.

Best regards,

YOU DON'T KNOW ME (2004)

You don't know me, but I know you. You don't know me, other than the sound of my voice and the image you have of me through your eyes, but I know your. I know you because I have been part of you since your beginning, not so long ago. I watched your early cries of frustration with this world you could not understand. I watched as you developed your sweet smile and gurgling sounds which later became words. I fed you through all of the stages, from baby bottle through solid food. I changed your diapers, bathed you and now help tie your shoes. I know you but you don't really know me. Yet. But you will. We will go through the stages where I am your hero, your playmate, and your answer man, the stage where my knowledge and judgment are severely questioned, on to the stage of lasting respect. And, possibly, finally, the stage where I won't know you. We will have been blest by what we know or what we knew.

THE LAKE THAT FLEW (1969)

(Co-Author Julie A Swift – Then Age 3)

Once upon a time, a long, long time ago, there was a beautiful spot in a far off country. The birds twittered in the forest and all the animals were happy there.

There was also a bad tempered mountain there and on all four sides of the bad tempered mountain were beautiful lakes. They had dark blue water and each was filled with happy fish. The larger lakes teased the smallest lake because she was so small and they were jealous of her because she was so beautiful.

The Lake Fairy Queen was happy with her beautiful spot in this far off country – even though the bad tempered mountain could be a problem, as could the jealousy of the largest lakes.

One day while the Lake Fairy Queen was away, the bad tempered mountain had a temper tantrum. Steam started coming out of the bad tempered mountain, then ash blotted out the sun, lava and huge rocks came down the mountainside and soon the largest lake was filled with rocks and lava. All the birds and animals were terrified because there were now only three lakes.

Another day while the Lake Fairy Queen was away, the bad tempered mountain had a temper tantrum. Steam started coming out of the bad tempered mountain, then ash blotted out the sun, lava and huge rocks came down the mountainside and soon this large lake was filled with rocks and lava. All the birds and animals were terrified because there were now only two lakes.

Again, while the Lake Fairy Queen was away, the bad tempered mountain had a temper tantrum. Steam started coming out of the bad tempered mountain, then ash blotted out the sun, lava and huge rocks came down the mountainside and soon this large lake was filled with rocks and lava. All the birds and animals were terrified because now only the beautiful small lake was left.

The smallest lake cried and cried and one day said to the Lake Fairy Queen, "What can I do? I know the bad tempered mountain – which even now was making gurgling noises, will fill me with rocks and lava the next time you have to be away. The birds and the animals will be so sad! Can you save me?"

The Lake Fairy Queen said, "I will try to work my magic and save you." That very night, when it was really dark, the Lake Fairy Queen said to the smallest lake, "Gather up your four corners like a big diaper and we will fly away!"

The smallest lake gathered up its four corners like a diaper, the Lake Fairy Queen took the corners and started to fly away with the lake. When they were over the volcano crater at the top of the bad tempered mountain, the Lake Fairy Queen dumped the lake into the crater. With a huge hissing sound, the bad tempered mountain quit causing trouble.

The smallest, most beautiful lake was now at the top of the mountain. The birds and the animals were happy again in the forest around the beautiful lake. The Lake Fairy Queen and the beautiful lake, which now was large and strong, just smiled and smiled.

SONGS

"Frog Pond" came into being because of conversations with Bob Shelton about a building lot his son had bought which had a frog pond on it. I never did get a recording of the frogs croaking so the words and music just happened.

FROG POND   (1998)

I'm smiling, I'm happy, I'm laughing out loud,

With my home in the country I feel so proud—

With a mailbox in front and a frog pond in back,

My heaven on earth is my tumble-down shack.

Frog pond, frog pond, sing your song to me;

Frog pond, frog pond, sing your song to me.

I'm frowning, I'm angry, I'm feeling plumb down,

The job that I have is the worst in this town—

Quittin' time's comin' is all I can say,

Then I'll be happy the rest of the day

Frog pond, frog pond, sing your song to me;

Frog pond, frog pond, sing your song to me.

It is a good thought but I do not remember exactly how this song came into being.

HELP ME BE HOLY (2007)

I am a sinner; I am so weak;

Always my pleasure is what I most seek.

I know my works, Lord, simply won't do—

I need your grace, Lord, to see me through.

Help me be holy, help me be pure,

Of my salvation, let me be sure.

I am a sinner, calling on You.

I need Your guidance in all that I do.

Thank you, dear Savior, who died on the tree

To carry the sin load of those such as me.

Help me be holy, help me be pure

Of my salvation, let me sure.

"Quittin" Time on the Railroad was my first song. My two young children and I were driving by the local railroad yards and I just started singing the first part of it. The melody seemed to fit and a few years later I completed the song.

QUITTIN' TIME ON THE RAILROAD (1979)

It's quittin' time on the railroad, quittin' time for today—

It's quittin' time on the railroad, where I work like a dog for my pay.

I want to go home and see Mary, but Mary don't live there no more—

I want to go home and hold Mary but she couldn't stand bein' poor.

She always hated my night work—it made her feel so alone.

She always hated my night work and it turned her heart to stone.

It's quittin' time on the railroad, quittin' time for today—

It's quittin' time on the railroad, where I work like a dog for my pay.

Mary started hittin' the night spots until my night's
work was through—

Mary started hittin' the night spots and that's where she
left me for you.

So I guess I'll go back to the tavern, a place where I've
already been—

I guess I'll go back to the tavern and start drinkin' all
over again.

For it's quittin' time on the railroad, quittin time for
today—

It's quittin' time on the railroad, where I work like a
dog for my pay.

"Golden Years" came easily: I had written a longer poem that gained some praise, then I extracted three verses and had these lyrics. The music came easily and just seemed to fit.

GOLDEN YEARS (2007)

The birds won't sing when my phone don't ring

As I sit here alone in my room—

An object of pity in this great city

My thoughts are shrouded in gloom.

Holy Spirit, Holy Spirit, I am counting on thee;

Holy Spirit, Holy Spirit, raise my prayers for me.

Why do I whine about this life of mine?

I really don't have a care.

My life isn't tough—I have more than enough

And I know that Jesus is there.

Holy Spirit, Holy Spirit, I am counting on thee;

Holy Spirit, Holy Spirit, raise my prayers for me.

I'll tell you the truth, I wasted my youth
And some of my later days.
This I shall do: be of service to You
And work at changing my ways.

Holy Spirit, Holy Spirit, I am counting on thee;
Holy Spirit, Holy Spirit, raise my prayers for me.

"Fam'ly and Friends" just came into being. The melody and words seemed to fit even though my job and my boss were fine.

FAM'LY AND FRIENDS (1981)

I've got a job that's driving me mad—

The work is so hard and the pay is so bad.

But I've got a gift sent from heaven above—

My wonderful life with the fam'ly I love.

Fam'ly and friends, yes, fam'ly and friends,

I thank the good Lord for my fam'ly and friends.

Now I've got a boss like Simon Legree—

I long for the day of him I'll be free.

And I've got few friends—they number just three—

But the ones that I have are a blessing to me.

Fam'ly and friends, yes, fam'ly and friends,

I thank the good Lord for my fam'ly and friends.

And I've got a God in heaven above.

He sent down His Son to show us his love.

While nailed to a cross He suffered and died—

I call him my Friend—He walks by my side.

Fam'ly and friends, yes, fam'ly and friends,

I thank the good Lord for my fam'ly and friends.

"I'm Gonna Get Even With You" was partially "inspired" by a bar scene I became aware of and the rest of it just like a possible slice of life.

I'M GONNA GET EVEN WITH YOU (1980)

Here I sit on my bar stool, alone and feelin' so blue,

Drinkin' down the courage to do what I'm wantin' to do.

It's been three years since I've been here and bad years they have been—

For I've done time in prison while she was livin' in sin.

So sing me a sad song just like the mood I'm in,

Sing me a sad song just like the place I've been;

Yes, sing me a sad song it's the least you can do—

And when you're done singin' I'm gonna get even with you.

Yes, I'm back at the place where it started—the place that ruined my life,

The place I brought my loved one who I wanted to be my wife.

And you were the barroom musician just as slick as you
could be—

After she first saw you, she no longer cared for me.

So sing me a sad song just like the mood I'm in,

Sing me a sad song just like the place I've been;

Yes, sing me a sad song it's the least you can do—

And when you're done singin' I'm gonna get even with
you.

"I Only Know My Heart Is Broke" is just a reflection of the often wrong feelings one has when a love affair goes wrong.

I ONLY KNOW MY HEART IS BROKE (1986)

Another dark and dismal day since you have gone
away;

Another long and sleepless night without you by my
side.

You've gone away, I don't know why, I only wish I
knew—

I only know my heart is broke and I am missing you.

I was born alone, I'll die alone, alone I'll always be.

No one can ever hope to know my lonesome misery.

You've gone away, I don't know why, I don't know
what I'll do—

I only know my heart is broke and I am missing you.

I only know my heart is broke and I am missing you.

56

"Our Rainbow" is another "poor me" song which reflects the feelings of one who believes they have been used poorly.

OUR RAINBOW (1984)

You said you would love me forever.

You said you would always be true.

You said like a beautiful rainbow

Your love would always shine through.

I said I would love you forever.

I said I would always be true.

I said 'til the end of forever

I'd love none other than you.

You say you now love another.

You say that our good love is through.

You say that our rainbow has faded,

For you now love somebody new.

I cried at the end of our rainbow.

I cried for the good times were done.

I cried for our beautiful rainbow

Had faded like mist in the sun.

Had faded like mist in the sun.

"There's A Light" was started as my family drove with our good friends in an area somewhere around Seminole, Florida. I noticed the street signs which are used in this song and the foundation of the song just announced itself.

THERE'S A LIGHT (1985)

There's a light in the window of a home far away

Where a mother so loving will silently pray.

She prays for her child who sings with a band

Near the light at the corner of Tenth Street and Grand.

Yes, there's a light on the corner of Tenth Street and Grand—

That lights up the barroom where I sing with the band

And brightens the shadows where the poor winos lay

As they drink their Sweet Lucy at the close of the day.

There's a light that is shining for you and for me—

It's the bright light of freedom in our great country.

And there's a light that is shining in heaven above

With a message of hope and peace and love.

And there's a light on the corner of Tenth Street and
Grand—

That lights up the barroom where I sing with the band

And brightens the shadows where the poor winos lay

As they drink their Sweet Lucy at the close of the day.

As they drink their Sweet Lucy at the close of the day.

"Song Of TheMountain Wind" was started as my

family was traveling with friends in Eastern

Tennessee and I saw a "Cumberland" sign.

SONG OF THE MOUNTAIN WIND (1980)

In Cumberland county where the mountain folk dwell

The wind in the pines has a story to tell.

It's honest and trusting and loving and true—

Is all of the story of my love for you.

But wicked and wild and fleeting and free

Tells all of the story of your love for me.

And the wind in the hollers blows gentle and mild

While the wind on the ridges blows wicked and wild

And the words to the music that makes up its song

Is, "Here in the mountains is a girl you done wrong."

In Cumberland county where the mountain winds blow

I set by my cabin where the Sweet Williams grow.

I'm lonely and sad and blue as can be—

I don't know what's gonna happen to me.

While you're in the city a-livin' so wild,

I'm here in the mountains a-carryin' your child.

And the wind in the hollers blows gentle and mild

While the wind on the ridges blows wicked and wild

And the words to the music that makes up its song

Is, "Here in the mountains is a girl you did wrong."

"Don't Cry Little Sister" is a protest song.
It was started because of my very strong
disagreement with court decisions which
allowed this child abuse to take place.

DON'T CRY LITTLE SISTER (1979)

Two little children got on
The school bus I drive;
It was the first day of school
And it felt good to be alive.

They sat in the seat right behind me
And it sure changed my day
When the little boy turned to his sister
And these words he did say:

Don't cry little sister, I love you.

And I know that don't mean much today.

But maybe some glad day tomorrow

They won't treat children this way.

Mama cried, too, little sister,

While she was talkin' to Dad.

She said she couldn't come get us

If we got to feelin' bad.

And she'd always fear for our safety

As off on the bus we would go

To attend a faraway school

For a reason she did not know.

"Benedict Arnold," Dad called him—

The Judge who ruled on the case.

He went on to say that he was

A disgrace to the whole human race.

And when one man has the power

To cause so much pain—

Then the patriots who died for our country

Did fight for our freedom in vain.

I know you're scared, little sister,

And I know the bus ride is long.

Yes, we've passed our neighborhood school—

I'm afraid that Judge was wrong.

Don't cry little sister, I love you.

And I know that don't mean much today.

But maybe some glad day tomorrow

They won't treat children this way.

Maybe some glad day tomorrow

They won't treat children this way.

"It's A Sometimes World" came about as *I was attempting to recognize the memory of a "sometimes shop" that Bob Shelton and I haphazardly operated some years earlier.*

IT'S A SOMETIMES WORLD (1989)

It's a sometimes world, a king once said—
She's not my queen—off with her head!
In this sometimes world, I'll tell you all,
We sometimes rise and we sometimes fall.

For it's a sometimes world sometimes sometimes
It's a sometimes world sometimes sometimes
It's a sometimes world sometimes sometimes
It's a sometimes world sometimes sometimes

In this sometimes world, my friend and I

Have a sometimes shop with things to buy.

Sometimes we're there and make a buck,

Sometimes we're gone and live on luck.

Chorus

It's a sometimes world, we all must say

When we have bills that we cannot pay.

For we all have times when things go wrong—

That's why we sing this little song

Chorus

"I've Got A Problem" is a problem: the

only problem was my thought that I

needed another song for the CD.

I'VE GOT A PROBLEM (2005)

I've got a problem, I've got a problem, I've got a
problem

I'm gonna share with you.

I am so lonely, I am so lonely, I am so lonely

I don't know what I'll do.

We could be happy

If you would kiss me

And hold me to your heart.

So why won't you hold me?

Why won't you kiss me?

Why must we stay apart?

I've got a problem, I've got a problem, I've got a
problem

I'm gonna share with you.

I am so lonely, I am so lonely, I am so lonely

I don't know what I'll do.

Two political activist friends and I
sang this for a Republican dinner
meeting. As you can see, names
have been replaced.

DON'T VOTE FOR A DEMMY (1988)

It's voting time in this country,

Voting time in this state,

It's voting time in this County—

So listen before it's too late!

Don't vote for a Demmy,

Don't vote for their liberal way!

Don't vote for a Demmy,

It's always the people who pay.

Do vote for old _____--

I pray you will listen to me.

Do vote for old _____--

For this State of the brave and the free!

Don't vote for a Demmy,

Don't fall for their pitiful tale!

Don't vote for a Demmy,

Like _____, _____, or _____.

For a time when I was in the Air Force

I had a real interest in Dixieland music.

I liked the song "St. James Infirmary Blues"

and this song of mine is a take-off on that.

The St. James Way is a pilgrimage trail across

Northern Spain that I walked with a small group

in 2005. We sang this one night.

ST. JAMES INFIRM BLUES (2005)

Walking alone on the old pilgrim trail—

I was sentenced to walk it or spend time in jail—

My feet are hurting, I keep falling down,

My kidneys are bursting, oh where's the next town?

The clothes on my back are ragged and worn,

The skin on my feet is ripped and torn,

My knees are hurting, my back black and blue,

My poor heart is breaking as I'm thinking of you.

My sins were forgiven at the old iron cross—

I'm sorry I stole money from my tight-fisted boss.

I may have been *muy, muy malo,* I want you to know—

Now all I can say is *"lo siento."* (I'm sorry.)

THE GOLDEN YEARS (2007)

The birds won't sing when my phone don't ring

as I sit here alone in my room.

An object of pity in this great city,

my thoughts are shrouded in gloom.

The shows on TV are an insult to me

and I'm too tired to vacuum or dust.

I want to cry as I wait to die,

living because I must.

My spirits are low as onward I go;

my mind is clouded with fog.

I forgot to say no mail today—

not even a catalog.

My cooking is bad when I'm feeling so sad

as I wait for heaven's call.

My bills are all paid but my bed is unmade—

as if that matters at all.

I am totally aghast as I look at my past

and know that I'm responsible for me.

I've plenty to read—more than I need,

and I live in the land of the free.

Why do I whine about this life of mine?

I really don't have a care.

My life isn't tough, I have more than enough

and I know that Jesus is there.

I'll tell you the truth, I wasted my youth

and some of my later days.

This I shall do, be of service to You

and work at changing my ways.

A DINNER DATE (1994)

I awaited her arrival with such anticipation

While reviewing her merits with much appreciation.

The coffee grew cold and finally undrinkable;

My thoughts turned sad—almost unthinkable.

I waited and waited and waited in vain,

Thinking perhaps she'd been struck by a train.

Or, like the others, I thought with a sigh,

She'd found another—more desirable than I.

Then later, much later, the frown left my face

As I saw my lady come into the place.

She said she'd been unavoidably delayed

My spirits then soared—no longer afraid.

ANOTHER DINNER DATE (1994)

"What makes you think that's not my car?"

I heard my lady say:

Her voice sounded "snippy"

At the end of this long, long day.

We'd finished our meal and paid for it

And left a generous tip:

She'd found her car and inserted the key

As we prepared for the homeward trip.

"I don't know why it won't unlock!"

She said with a puzzled frown.

"It seems I've left the lights on

And it's run the battery down."

"Well it WON'T unlock," she snarled into the phone

When told that the battery didn't matter.

"Just come here soon, prepared to break in

And stop this idle chatter!"

With an hour to wait for service

We sat in the moonlit lot.

The better to see her errant car,

I'd moved mine to a closer spot.

I glanced at the car we'd tried to unlock

And stared hard at the license plate.

Then said "You better cancel the service call

Before it is too late.

"What makes you think that's not my car?"

She said—in the voice I hate to hear—

I pointed to another row, and softly said,

"Your car is over here."

All's well that ends well,

I've heard it often said—

She cancelled the call and we each went home

(But her face was mighty red).

A PERFORMANCE CITATION (1994)

We have all failed to perform

As we've struggled through this life—

Some with a husband so dear,

Others with a wife.

Some have failed to perform

In a job that was so hard.

Some have met with no success

Tending a stubborn yard.

A burst of pride swells in my heart

As I take this time to say

My lady was awarded a performance citation

As recently as yesterday.

"Good morning, officer," were the words

She spoke with a little grin—

Knowing full well as she sat there

That she was guilty as sin.

"Fifty-two in a thirty," he said.

"You've got to hold it down—

We don't allow such driving

In our gentle Quaker town."

"It was the fault of the talk show host!

As he praised the liberal kind

I tromped on the gas in anger—

I guess I lost my mind."

"If I were the judge I'd say 'not guilty'—

Of that please have no fear.

But let me present this performance citation

To make my position clear."

A BRACELET IOU (1995)

The shopping time does so swiftly go—

Delayed by flat tires, sleet and snow—

And now it's gone. You leave tomorrow—

And I a present short, to my sorrow.

It seems the least that I should do—

Is present you with this IOU.

We'll shop again—where'er they're sold

'Til I find the perfect band of gold—

And then you'll think I'm truly great—

And forgive me fully for being late.

RUBYE DEAR (2007)

Oh, Rubye dear I lived in fear

That you would fade away

And leave me alone with a heart of stone

Just living from day to day.

Yet time went by and happy was I

For a number of blissful years;

But bad times came, cancer was the name,

That turned our smiles to tears.

The doctors were great and delayed her fate

And she was strong and brave.

Then the death angel came and called her name

With the voice that leads to the grave.

The winds do moan as I sit here alone.

Yes, all alone with my heart of stone.

CHRISTMAS SNACKS FROM JULIE (2006)

With never a thought of all the calories

or calls of "there goes the fat man" from the galleries,

I sample them all in utmost haste—

never a morsel will I waste.

First, a crinkly gourmet chip

slathered with tasty onion dip.

Next, a cracker flavored with sesame,

then some hot dried peas called wasabi.

Polish chocolate and other candy

I must describe as simply dandy.

Hot wasabi beans in a jar,

cans of nuts—the best there are.

Caramel corn and other treats—

I'll sample each—and then the meats!

Happy am I, her old Dad—

She's the best daughter I ever had.

MEMORIAL DAY (2008)

Many were called and most of us went,

Having no choice as to where we were sent.

Marching and training all the long day,

Doing it all for minimal pay.

Graduation came with its required parade,

Assignments were coming and most were afraid.

Will I be sent to the front lines to serve?

When it comes to killing will I lack the nerve?

Those who returned were torn and tattered,

Wondering how much their sacrifice mattered.

The appeasers in the party politic,

We must admit, just make us sick.

And we find we want to shout,

Help us throw the bastards out!

TV LOVE (2008)

Visiting with family miles away,

I watched the food channel every day

hoping to improve my cooking skill,

which all these lessons surely will.

Later, overnighting at the Ramada,

my thoughts turned to my Giada

and our love which could not be

for she cared not a whit for me.

Imagination is a wonderful thing,

causing our hearts and minds to sing—

but reality comes, to my sorrow—

so, what's on the menu for tomorrow?

Cooking skill is no big deal—

think I'll fix—instant oatmeal!

MUSINGS OF AN OLD MAN (2008)

Today you and the grandkids came to town,

I needed that—I was feeling down.

I wish I had a place where you could stay,

I wish you didn't live so far away,

I wish my food was halfway good—

I'd do much better if I could.

I know I should adjust my attitude

And continue my life with gratitude.

As for today, I'm feeling glad—

I've the best children that ever man had.

Perhaps I've expected too much of life—

A decent job and a loving wife.

THE VOICE (2008)

I was all alone in a crowded room

And my heart was down and full of gloom.

It seemed that troubles and sorrows were my lot

And that troubles and trials were all I got.

Relationships and money had all gone away

And now I had debts that I could not pay.

Then I said a short prayer so silently;

Praying for guidance and direction for me.

Then a voice came down from the Lord above:

"Do not worry now—you still have my love.

For my Son I sent that you might live

No greater gift could I ever give.

There's only one thing that you must do—

Just live your life as He tells you to."

PRETTY RUTH (2008)

When I was young and really stupid

I felt an arrow shot by Cupid;

There was so much I did not know

But I could not control my libido.

So, there I was on bended knee

Asking Pretty Ruth to marry me.

The first years went by in a blur

And I mostly got along with her.

The Air Force then became my duty,

So I left behind my raving beauty.

Months later came the "Dear John" letter;

She thought she'd found someone better.

Ruthless was I for a span

Then I became another's man.

AT FIFTY (1990)

When one has labored under the sun

For years that total forty-nine and one,

Served their fellow when they could

And read the Good Book as they should—

Just like Solomon they will see

All, yes all, is vanity.

AT FIFTY-ONE (1991)

Seasons come and seasons go,

Summer sun and winter snow,

In the fall and then the spring,

Falling leaves and birds that sing.

Seasons come to mortals too:

Even me, and, more so, you.

Days of sorrow, days of song,

Swiftly, swiftly speed along.

Childhood days of perfect bliss,

Teenage years and that first kiss.

Soon the twenties go drifting by,

Thirty comes, and some folk cry.

Though it's often said, it's just not so,

Life doesn't begin when you hit four-oh.

Just as often it's been told

Fifty means "you're getting old."

When you arrive at one and fifty,

No matter if you're feeling "nifty,"

It pains me much to have to say—

"You're over the hill; you've had your day."

BLESSINGS (2006)

The covered porch is nice and dry

As I watch the rain come from the sky

Thinking my God is so good to me

Providing blessings I can see

While drinking coffee and eating pie.

AGING (2006)

If one reaches ten plus three score

They may be rich or they may be poor

They may have grandchildren at their knee

A force at work they may no longer be

They must not stop; they must do more.

STUPID EDITOR (2006)

Scribbling words with pen and ink

Ideas seem to come in a blink

Through the words the editor fans

Some approved, some he pans

Saying "this doth truly stink."

SOCCER GIRL (2006)

Long hair flying in the breeze

Handling the ball with graceful ease

Scarcely aware of the watching crowd

Cheering long and cheering loud

The task at hand is all she sees.

PLAY

JUDGMENT DAY (2008)

A One-Act Christian Play

By Linden H. Swift

CAST, ATTIRE, DESCRIPTIONS

GOD: white robe, a shiny gold covering over His face

JESUS: white robe, slim, small beard and moustache

RECORDING ANGEL: white robe, wings, halo

FOUR ESCORTING ANGELS: white robes, wings, halos

FIRST SINNER: a dark male, white robe, head covering

SECOND SINNER: a trim woman, 35 to 40, short skirt, high heels

THIRD SINNER: a clean-cut man, perhaps 40, suit and tie

FOURTH SINNER: an elderly man, priestly robe, appropriate headdress

FIFTH SINNER: a slight, poorly dressed, older woman

SIXTH SINNER: a slightly overweight, nice-appearing man, aged about 60

SEVENTH SINNER: an old man, flowing robe

EIGHTH SINNER: a sharply dressed black man, aged about 60

SETTING

The stage is bare except for a long table, two chairs and a kneeler.

GOD occupies one chair with JESUS occupying the one to His right.

The kneeler faces the end of the table to the right of GOD.

Two large books are on the end of the table to the left of GOD.

The RECORDING ANGEL is at the end of the table, the books directly in front of him.

The ESCORTING ANGELS and the SINNERS will enter from stage right.

Behind the RECORDING ANGEL is a stairway going up to a door which is the entry to heaven. When this door is opened the sounds of the "Hallelujah Chorus" come forth.

Also behind the RECORDING ANGEL, steps lead down to the door which is the entry to hell. When this door is opened, screams, groans and sounds of sorrow come forth.

SCENE ONE

GOD: {*Turning toward RECORDING ANGEL.*} We may start now.

RECORDING ANGEL: {*Calls to stage right.*} Bring out the First Sinner.

{*Two ESCORTING ANGELS escort the FIRST SINNER to the kneeler; he kneels, face down. The E.A.s take a step back.*}

R.A.: {*To SINNER.*} What did you do with the talents you were given?

FIRST SINNER: {*Sits up.*} I served my God as I was taught, promoted this belief to the best of my ability and thoroughly hated and persecuted those who did not believe as I do.

R.A. {*Facing GOD and JESUS, consults the books.*} The Book of Sins lists him as being guilty of the sin of anger and his name does not appear in The Book of Life.

GOD: {*To SINNER.*} You are a sinner and I hate sin. {*Turns toward JESUS and motions for comment.*}

JESUS: {*To GOD.*} I knew him not.

GOD: {*To E.A.s.*} Cast him down!

FIRST SINNER: {*Being escorted to the Gates of Hell.*}
Mercy! Mercy! I did as I was taught! Spare me!

{*The door is opened, sounds come forth and he is
pushed in. E.A.s exit stage left and return, backstage, to
stage right.*}

SCENE TWO

RECORDING ANGEL: {*To stage right.*} Bring out the Second Sinner.

{*Two ESCORTING ANGELS escort the SECOND SINNER to the kneeler; she kneels, face down. The E.A.s take a step back.*}

R.A: {*To SINNER.*} What did you do with the talents you were given?

SECOND SINNER: {*Sits up.*} Feeling that God loves me regardless of my actions, I tried to love all the men I met—particularly if they were rich.

R.A.: {*Facing GOD and JESUS, consults the books.*} The Book of Sins shows her to be guilty of the sin of adultery. While thinking most about how to gratify the desires of her sinful nature she also attempted to alienate her children from their father. Her name does not appear in The Book of Life.

GOD: {*To SINNER.*} You are a sinner and I hate sin.{*Turns toward JESUS and motions for comment.*}

JESUS: {*To GOD.*} I knew her not.

GOD: {*To E.A.s.*} Cast her down!

SECOND SINNER: {*Being escorted to the Gates of Hell.*} Mercy! Mercy! I am not all bad! This is, like, not fair!

{*The door is opened, sounds come forth and she is pushed in. E.A.s exit stage left and return, backstage, to stage right.*}

SCENE THREE

RECORDING ANGEL: {*Calls to stage right.*} Bring out the Third Sinner.

{*Two ESCORTING ANGELS escort the THIRD SINNER to the kneeler; he kneels, face down. The E.A.s take a step back.*}

R.A: {*To SINNER.*} What did you do with the talents you were given?

THIRD SINNER: {*Sits up.*} I always attempted to take care of my many obligations and perhaps overcompensated to my children for the actions of their mother. I am a repentant, baptized sinner and I know that Jesus carried my sin load for me.

R.A: {*Facing GOD and JESUS, consults the books.*} His name does not appear in The Book of Sins and 'diligence' appears by his name in The Book of Life.

GOD: {*To SINNER.*} You are a sinner and I hate sin. {*Turns toward JESUS and motions for comment.*}

JESUS: {*To GOD.*} He is one of Mine, Father.

GOD: {*To E.A.s.*} Take him to be welcomed home.

THIRD SINNER: {*Being escorted to Heaven's door, repeatedly shouts.*} Praise   God! Thank you, Jesus!

{Shouts of welcome and the Hallelujah Chorus sound as the door is opened. E.A.s exit stage left and return, backstage, to stage right.}

SCENE FOUR

RECORDING ANGEL: {*Calls to stage right.*} Bring out the Fourth Sinner.

{*Two ESCORTING ANGELS escort the FOURTH SINNER to the kneeler; he kneels, face down. The E.A.s take a step back.*}

R.A: {*To SINNER.*} What did you do with the talents you were given?

FOURTH SINNER: {*Sits up.*} I was the leader of a large religious body. I directed the hierarchy and left my successor a great storehouse of treasure.

R.A: {*Facing GOD and JESUS, consults the books.*} The sin of greed is associated with his name in The Book of Sins and he thought much about gratifying his sinful nature.His name does not appear in The Book of Life.

GOD: {*To SINNER.*} You are a sinner and I hate sin. {*Turns toward JESUS and motions for comment.*}

JESUS: {*To GOD.*} I knew him not.

GOD: {*To E.A.s.*} Cast him down!

FOURTH SINNER: {*Being escorted to the Gates of Hell.*} Mercy! Mercy! Give me another chance! {*The door is opened, sounds come forth and he is pushed in.*}

E.A.s exit stage left and return, backstage, to stage right.}

SCENE FIVE

RECORDING ANGEL: {*Calls to stage right.*} Bring out the Fifth Sinner.

{*Two ESCORTING ANGELS escort the FIFTH SINNER to the kneeler; she kneels, face down. The E.A.s take a step back.*}

R.A.: {*To SINNER.*} What did you do with the talents you were given?

FIFTH SINNER: {*Sits up.*} My accomplishments were few. I was widowed at an early age and was responsible for our three small children. We never had much money and I was unable to contribute much. I directed my children to the best of my ability, did volunteer work when I could and was a baptized believer.

R.A: {*Facing GOD and JESUS, consults the books.*} Her name does not appear in The Book of Sins. 'Patience' is listed as her primary virtue in The Book of Life.

GOD: {*To SINNER.*} You are a sinner and I hate sin. {*Turns toward JESUS and motions for comment.*}

JESUS: {*To GOD.*} She is one of Mine, Father.

GOD: {*To E.A.s.*} Take her to be welcomed home.

FIFTH SINNER: {*Being escorted to Heaven's door, repeatedly shouts.*} Praise God! Thank you, Jesus! {*Shouts of welcome and the Hallelujah Chorus sound as the door is opened. E.A.s exit stage left and return, backstage, to stage right.*}

SCENE SIX

RECORDING ANGEL: {*Calls to stage right.*} Bring out the Sixth Sinner.

{*Two ESCORTING ANGELS escort the SIXTH SINNER to the kneeler; he kneels, face down. The E.A.s step back.*}

R.A.: {*To SINNER.*} What did you do with the talents you were given?

SIXTH SINNER: {*Sits up.*} I was a very well-known and popular political leader who did much for my people and my country. I was well loved practically throughout the world. I often attended church and was welcome in many congregations.

R.A.: {*Facing GOD and JESUS, consults the books.*} The sin of lust is associated with his name in The Book of Sins. He thought much about gratifying his sinful desires.His name does not appear in The Book of Life.

GOD: {*To SINNER.*} You are a sinner and I hate sin. {*Turns toward JESUS and motions for comment.*}

JESUS: {*To GOD.*} I knew him not.

GOD: {*To E.A.s.*} Cast him down!

SIXTH SINNER: {*Being escorted to the Gates of Hell, repeatedly shouts.*} Mercy! Mercy! Mercy! I did so much! What else could you want?

{*The door is opened, sounds come forth and he is pushed in. E.A.s exit stage left and return, backstage, to stage right.*}

SCENE SEVEN

RECORDING ANGEL: {*Calls to stage right.*} Bring out the Seventh Sinner.

{*Two ESCORTING ANGELS escort the SEVENTH SINNER to the kneeler; he kneels, face down. The E.A.s take a step back.*}

R.A. {*To SINNER.*} What did you do with the talents you were given?

SEVENTH SINNER: {*Sits up.*} For over fifty years I served as a missionary in a very undeveloped country. There was much anti-Christian sentiment there but, thanks be to God, I made some inroads. I tried hard to accomplish more. I was not without sin but, through Jesus, I was forgiven.

R.A.: {*Facing GOD and JESUS, consults the books.*} His name does not appear in The Book of Sins and 'humility' is listed as his primary virtue in The Book of Life.

GOD: {*To SINNER.*} You are a sinner and I hate sin.

{*Turns toward JESUS and motions for comment.*}

JESUS: {*To GOD.*} He is one of Mine, Father.

GOD: {*To E.A.s.*} Take him to be welcomed home.

SEVENTH SINNER: {*Being escorted to Heaven's door, repeatedly shouts.*} Praise God! Thank you, Jesus!

{*Shouts of welcome and the Hallelujah Chorus sound as the door is opened. E.A.s exit stage left and return, backstage, to stage right.*}

SCENE EIGHT

RECORDING ANGEL: {*Calls to stage right.*} Bring out the Eighth Sinner.

{*Two ESCORTING ANGELS escort the EIGHTH SINNER to the kneeler; he kneels, face down. The E.A.s take a step back.*}

R.A.: {*To SINNER.*} What did you do with the talents you were given?

EIGHTH SINNER: {*Sits up.*} I was a social activist for my God-fearing people. I accomplished many good things for them. I was called 'Reverend,' even though I did not actually lead a congregation. My people adored me.

R.A.: {*Facing GOD and JESUS, consults the books.*} The sin of pride is associated with his name in The Book of Sins and he thought most often about gratifying his sinful   desires. His name does not appear in The Book of Life.

GOD: {*To SINNER.*} You are a sinner and I hate sin.

{*Turns toward JESUS and motions for comment.*}

JESUS: {*To GOD.*} I knew him not.

GOD: {*To E.A.s.*} Cast him down!

EIGHTH SINNER: {*Being escorted to the Gates of Hell, repeatedly shouts.*} This is not fair—I did so much! Grant me mercy!

{*The door is opened, sounds come forth and he is pushed in. E.A.s exit stage left.*}

JESUS: {*Lifting His hand to interrupt R.A.*} Father, I tire of this discouragement. Shall We not now walk in the cool of the garden for a time?

GOD: As You wish, My Son.

{*All other action stops, GOD and JESUS arise and walk, arm in arm, to the stairs which lead to Heaven's gate.*}

THE CURTAIN FALLS

IN MEMORIAM

A TRUE STORY (1994)

By Edna Swift Northerner

O'Reilly's son, Patrick, and Bridget O'Leary
Since childhood had known what they wanted in life;
Of dreaming and planning they never grew weary –
They'd go to the New World when she was his wife.

For long years they labored, a-scrimping and saving,
Though kin in America sent what they could,
And neither complained of the working and slaving,
Convinced that 'twas needful and for their own good.

At last they had scraped enough money together
To pay for their passage and give them a start.
Their one grief was saying their farewells forever
To Ireland and loved ones from whom they must part.

'twas April when Father O'Shaughnessy wed them;

From Queenstown they sailed, in the County of Cork,

Pursuing the dream that had finally led them

Aboard the Titanic and bound for New York.

PENNSYLVANIA DRUMMER BOY (1994)

By Edna Swift Northerner

When our militia went to fight the redcoats late that summer,

Old Abie Schwartz was real bad sick and couldn't be their
drummer;

So our John Thomas went along – he'd learned the beats from
Abie.

John Thomas was our youngest son, not much more than a baby.

My man and older boys went too, along with all the others –

Our neighbor men and other kin – four nephews and two
brothers.

I watched them march off down the road while Johnny beat the
measure.

And how he strutted! Straight and proud, his face all flushed with
pleasure.

They soon joined up with Gen'ral Wayne, were beaten at Paoli,

And just one son came limpin' home to tell me sadly, slowly,

My man and other sons were dead, killed in the battle's fury:

Except John Thomas – he'd marched on. Said tell me not to
worry.

Eight years went past; my crippled son looked out and saw him comin:

A white-haired old man stumblin' home a-bawlin' like a woman.

Gone was my pretty drummer boy, so full of life and promise.

Gone , just the same as if he'd died. My baby! My John Thomas.

END OF BOOK 1

MAKING MEALS, MANAGING MONEY,

AND LIVING LIFE

Consulting Editor Sharon Herbitter

Printed by Augustin Printers, Richmond, IN

LINDENWOULD PUBLISHING CO. INC.

BOX 203 PLAINFIELD, IN 46168-0203

CONTENTS

FOREWORD

You do not really need this book if you have no problem preparing simple meals, money management at your current and anticipated future income levels is of no concern, and your relationships and those whom you care about could not be better. Almost certainly you know a person whose life will be enriched if you will purchase this book for them. Of course, I may not be looking at this objectively.

Linden H. Swift   summer 2010

In addition to the above, the following words by Sharon Herbitter appeared on the back cover of the print edition: "Those of us who have become fans of Linden's wit and wisdom will be delighted with this new offering. A mixture of advice: much of it sound, some of it made with tongue firmly planted in cheek (and it's up to you to decide which is which!). I chuckled and contemplated my way through his latest book, making some notes of things I want to be sure to pass along to my son."

MAKING MEALS INTRODUCTION

Certainly, since she suffered the most, this section should be dedicated to my daughter, Julie. Almost uncomplainingly, she suffered through some of the worst cooking ever foisted off on an innocent person by a totally inept cook.

It was a bleak (in more ways than one) day in the fall of 1983 when my 16-year-old daughter and I discussed how we would handle the absence of mother and wife. It was decided that she, an extremely busy high school junior, would be responsible for the housekeeping tasks and I would attempt to become an adequate cook. I failed!

At this time, I was able to brew coffee, serve dry cereal, and, perhaps, make toast. These knowledge and ability limitations were amplified by my absolute inability to think—my mind was numb. This condition lasted for at least eighteen months and perhaps longer. Also, this new family situation resulted in a severe money shortage which dictated that we eat what I would prepare and rarely treat ourselves to a restaurant meal. The money shortage persisted for about six years. Fortunately for my son, Brian, he was attending college and rarely suffered through the torture I was dispensing.

The turning point may have begun some months later when Julie and I had occasion to weigh ourselves. She, with a normal weight of maybe 108 pounds now weighed just 82 pounds. I, normally at 198 was a good forty pounds lighter. Learning to cook can be quite difficult for some.

Enough of that! Let us now advance to the present day: both children lived through this difficult time and I, living alone, am usually not unhappy with the food I prepare. I use an electric stove with an oven, a toaster oven, a microwave, a graniteware slow cooker, and a tabletop electric grill as my cooking tools.

The following recipes are not complex, are usually for one meal for one person, and, on occasion, may allow for leftovers for a guest. I encourage you to develop a system of identifying those recipes to which you wish to return. Also, you should mix and match as you see fit. Now, start your education.

CHILI 1

½ lb. ground beef

1 15-oz. can diced tomatoes

1 15-oz. can chili beans

½ can water

3 tbsp. chili powder

Brown meat in cooking pot, drain off excess grease (not in sink), add other ingredients, boil gently 15 minutes, simmer 45 minutes, serve.

CHILI 2

½ lb. ground beef

1 15-oz. can diced tomatoes

1 15-oz. can chili beans

1 can water

4 tbsp. chili powder

¼ lb. pasta

Brown meat in cooking pot, drain off excess grease (not in sink), add other ingredients, boil gently 15 minutes, simmer 45 minutes, serve.

SLOW COOKER RUMP ROAST

1 lb. roast

1 or 2 potatoes, peeled and quartered

2 or 3 carrots, peeled and quartered

½ cup water

salt and pepper to taste

Place vegetables and water in bottom of graniteware slow cooker, add roast and water. Add salt and pepper shortly before serving. Cook on low for 8 or 9 hours.

OVEN BEEF RUMP ROAST

1 lb. rump roast

salt and pepper to taste

1 tbsp. prepared mustard

½ tsp. rosemary, optional

Place roast fat side up on rack in a small roasting pan. Add salt, pepper and, if desired, rosemary. Cover top of roast with mustard. Bake at 325 for 1 hour and 15 minutes. Let sit 10 minutes before slicing.

SPAGHETTI AND MEATBALLS

¼ lb. pasta

6 frozen purchased meatballs

1 cup purchased spaghetti sauce

1 tbsp. parmesan cheese (optional)

Prepare pasta according to package directions. Heat meatballs and sauce in saucepan, add cheese if desired. Serve meat sauce over pasta.

CANNED CHILI WITH RICE

1 15-oz. can chili with beans

4 tbsp. grape jelly

6 frozen purchased meatballs

½ cup quick cooking rice

½ cup water

Defrost meatballs, add to chili and jelly, bring to a slow boil.

Prepare rice according to package directions. Serve chili mixture over rice.

COFFEED RUMP ROAST

1 lb. rump roast

1 tsp. garlic powder

salt and pepper to taste

vinegar and black coffee

Marinate roast in mixture of coffee and vinegar for 12 hours. Place meat in small roasting pan, punch holes in top of roast, sprinkle top with garlic powder, almost cover roast with coffee, simmer 6 hours, press salt and pepper into roast, bring to boil, serve.

MEATBALLS WITH RICE

6 frozen purchased meatballs

12 oz. chili sauce

¾ cup grape jelly

¾ cup each quick cooking rice and water

Place meatballs, sauce, and jelly in covered pot, simmer for 2 hours then bring to boil. Serve over rice which has been prepared according to package directions.

CHUCK ROAST

1 ½ lb. chuck roast

1 tsp. pepper

1 tsp. garlic powder

water

Sprinkle and press in pepper and garlic powder on both sides of roast. Cook on top of stove in covered pot. Water should almost cover roast. Bring to boil for 10 minutes then simmer for 2 hours.

ROUND STEAK AND RICE

Serving-size piece of steak

1 tbsp. flour

2 tbsp. shortening

1 small onion, diced

½ cup water

1 10-oz. can cream of mushroom soup

¼ cup quick cooking rice with water

Pound flour into both sides of steak. Brown steak and onion in shortening, add water and soup. Simmer 1 hour, remove meat, bring liquid to boil, add rice, fluff and serve.

BAKED BACON-WRAPPED BEEF FILLET 1

1 bacon-wrapped fillet

Preheat oven to 375. Place the fillet on baking sheet and bake for 30 minutes. Serve.

BAKED BACON-WRAPPED BEEF FILLET 2

1 bacon-wrapped fillet

Preferably in a cast iron skillet, sear both sides of the fillet until it is quite brown. Place in 375 oven for 12 minutes. Serve. Skillet handle will be quite hot.

SAUERKRAUT AND WIENERS

1 15-oz. can sauerkraut

3 wieners

Place wieners in bottom of saucepan, cover with sauerkraut. Cover and bring to a slow boil, then simmer for another 20 minutes. Serve over mashed potatoes.

BEANS AND WIENERS

1 15-oz. can baked beans

4 wieners

3 tbsp. barbecue sauce

water

Cut wieners into bite-size pieces, boil for 5 minutes, drain, add beans and barbecue sauce, bring to a boil, then simmer for a few minutes.

ROAST BEEF MANHATTAN

1 slice bread

leftover beef to cover bread

1 serving instant mashed potatoes

1 serving gravy

Heat the beef, prepare mashed potatoes according to package directions, layer on plate according to above sequence. Either use purchased gravy or make gravy from packaged mix according to package directions.

MEAT LOAF

1 lb. ground beef

¼ small onion, chopped

1 cup crushed cracker crumbs

1 cup milk

1 tbsp. melted margarine or butter

1 egg, beaten

½ tsp. each salt and pepper

½ cup catsup

2 tbsp. brown sugar

Thoroughly mix all ingredients except catsup and brown sugar. Place mixture in loaf pan, mix catsup and brown sugar and cover top of loaf with this mixture. Bake at 350 for 1 ½ hours.

SLOW COOKER CHICKEN

1 chicken

1 tsp. each salt and pepper

1 tsp. basil

Rinse and pat dry one whole chicken. Place basil, salt, and pepper in cavity. Place in graniteware slow cooker, cook on high for 1 hour and on low for an additional 7 hours. Serve. Liquid should be saved for soup and leftover chicken saved for other dishes.

CORN AND CHICKEN CASSEROLE

½ 15-oz. can creamed corn

½ 15-oz. can whole kernel corn

1 cup leftover chicken, shredded

1 egg, beaten

1 tbsp. margarine, melted

½ tsp. salt

½ cup milk

½ box (4+ oz.) corn muffin mix

Mix first 7 ingredients in baking dish or pan, press muffin mix on top until moistened. Bake at 350 for 45 minutes.

CHICKEN AND NOODLES

1 ½ cups shredded leftover chicken

1 ½ cups egg noodles

2 ½ cups water

1 chicken-flavored bouillon cube

dash of salt

parmesan or romano cheese, optional

Place chicken, bouillon cube, and water in cooking pot. Cover and bring to a boil for 5 minutes. Stir in egg noodles and boil for another 5 minutes, stirring frequently. Place in serving bowls, sprinkle on cheese if desired and serve.

BAKED CHICKEN 1

1 chicken leg quarter

¾ cup crushed corn flakes or bread crumbs

½ cup Italian dressing

Marinate chicken in dressing for 2 hours, roll in flakes or crumbs and bake, covered, at 350 for 1 and ½ hours.

CHICKEN A LA KING

¼ small onion, diced

¼ cup butter or margarine

1 cup leftover shredded chicken

1 10-oz. can cream of mushroom soup

½ can milk

1 warm biscuit

Place butter or margarine and onion in medium skillet, sauté for a few minutes, add chicken, soup, and milk, bring to a slow boil for a few minutes. Crumble biscuit in serving plate and cover with skillet contents.

CHICKEN RICE SOUP

1 chicken leg quarter

3 cups salted water

6 baby carrots, cut to bite size

¾ cup quick cooking rice

In covered pot, boil chicken for 2 hours, remove and discard skin and bones, add carrots and rice, boil for a minute, let stand 5 minutes, fluff and serve.

CHICKEN VEGETABLE SOUP 1

1 chicken leg quarter

4 cups water

1 lb. frozen mixed vegetables

salt and pepper to taste

½ tsp. basil, optional

In covered pot boil chicken for 2 hours, remove and discard skin and bones, add other ingredients, boil gently for 30 or 45 minutes. Serve.

CHICKEN VEGETABLE SOUP 2

Liquid from slow cooker prepared chicken

Water if needed

1 cup shredded leftover chicken

1 lb. frozen mixed vegetables

1 chopped onion

Mix ingredients, bring to boil then simmer for 30 additional minutes.

CHICKEN WITH TOMATOES AND RICE

1 15-oz. can diced tomatoes

1 cup shredded leftover chicken

1 tbsp. minced garlic

1 tsp. pepper

¾ cup water

¾ cup quick cooking rice

Place first 5 ingredients in cooking pot, cover and bring to a boil, stir in rice, remove from heat, after 5 minutes fluff and eat.

PARMESAN CHICKEN

1 cup shredded leftover chicken

1 cup spaghetti sauce

2 tbsp. grated parmesan cheese

Place chicken in a small baking dish, mix sauce and cheese, pour over chicken, bake at 350 for 15 minutes and serve.

BAKED CHICKEN 2

1 chicken leg quarter

1 10-oz. can cream of mushroom soup

Place chicken in baking dish, cover chicken with soup, cover and bake at 350 for 1 ¼ hours. Serve.

CHICKEN SALAD

¾ cup shredded leftover chicken

3 tbsp. salad dressing or mayonnaise

dash of garlic powder and of lemon pepper

Heat chicken, mix with other ingredients, serve on bread or crackers.

SALMON PATTIES

1 15-oz. can salmon, drained

½ cup bread crumbs

1 egg

dash of pepper

Thoroughly mix ingredients, form into 4 or 5 patties, fry in oil about 5 minutes on each side until nicely browned.

TUNA CASSEROLE

1 10 oz. can cream of mushroom soup

½ cup milk

1 cup frozen peas

1 6-oz. can of tuna

2 cups cooked egg noodles

1 oz. shredded cheese

Stir first 5 ingredients into a loaf pan, bake at 400 for 30 minutes, stir in cheese, bake 10 more minutes.

HAM AND GREEN BEANS AND POTATOES

1 6-oz. cooked ham slice, diced

1 15-oz. can green beans

1 potato, chunked

Mix all ingredients in saucepan, cook on medium heat for 25 minutes or until potatoes are tender. Simmer another 30 minutes.

FRIED HAM SLICE

1 6-oz. cooked ham slice

1 tbsp. prepared mustard

1 tbsp. brown sugar

Spread mustard and sprinkle sugar on top of slice. Fry over medium heat about 6 minutes per side.

PINEAPPLE HAM

1 6-oz. cooked ham slice

5 tbsp. crushed pineapple

Place ham in small baking dish, cover with pineapple, cover and bake at 325 for 20 minutes.

HAM WITH SWEET POTATOES

1 6-oz. cooked ham slice, diced

1 15-oz. can sweet potatoes

½ cup quick cooking rice, prepared

2 tbsp. brown sugar

Mix all ingredients and bake at 350 for 25 minutes.

HAM AND BEANS

1 6-oz. cooked ham slice, diced

1 30-oz. can pinto beans

¼ cup water

1 onion, diced

½ tsp. oregano

Place ingredients in covered saucepan, bring to slow boil, then simmer for 30 minutes. Stir occasionally and do not let all liquid cook away.

HAM CASSEROLE

1 8-oz. cooked ham slice, diced

15-oz. can peas

2 cups cooked rice

1 chopped onion

1 10-oz. can cheddar cheese soup

½ cup shredded cheese

½ cup milk

dash of basil, garlic powder, and pepper

Mix and bake, covered, at 375 for 40 minutes.

PORK ROAST

1 3-lb. pork picnic

1 tbsp. minced garlic

¼ cup water

2 potatoes, quartered

salt and pepper

Rub the roast with salt and pepper, bake in oven at 375 for 30 minutes, pour off grease (not in sink), place water and onions in bottom of graniteware slow cooker, add roast, potatoes and garlic. Cook on low for 9 hours.

FRIED PORK CHOPS

2 pork chops

mix a bit of flour, garlic salt, and pepper

1 tbsp. cooking oil

Dust the mixture over both sides of the chops, brown chops on both sides, cook over medium heat, covered, for about 10 minutes on each side.

BARBECUED RIBS

2 lbs. meaty ribs

1 cup barbecue sauce

Place ribs in graniteware slow cooker, cover with sauce, cook on low for 9 hours.

BARBECUED RIBS AND RICE

leftover barbecued ribs

½ cup each quick cooking rice and water

small amount of barbecue sauce

In small saucepan prepare rice according to package directions, fluff, add heated meat and barbecue sauce.

PORK RIB, SAUERKRAUT, AND POTATO

1 small western cut pork rib

1 15-oz. can sauerkraut

1 medium-size potato, chunked

In graniteware slow cooker place potato in bottom, add rib and cover with sauerkraut. Cover, cook on low for 9 hours.

SMOKED SAUSAGE DISH

¼ lb. smoked sausage

1 large potato, diced

1 cup chopped cabbage

4 cups water

pepper

Cut link sausage into bite-size pieces, place all ingredients in saucepan, bring to boil, reduce heat, simmer another 30 minutes .

SMOKED SAUSAGE AND BAKED BEANS

1 16-oz. can baked beans

2 small potatoes, diced after microwaving

4 oz. smoked sausage links, bite sized

1 tbsp. minced garlic

Place all ingredients in saucepan, bring to slow boil, then simmer for about 15 minutes. Do not let all liquid boil away; you may need to add a small amount of water.

SAUERKRAUT AND SMOKED SAUSAGE

4 oz. smoked link sausage, cut to bite size

15-oz. can sauerkraut

Place in covered pan, bring to boil, after 5 minutes reduce heat and simmer for 15 minutes. Serve over mashed potatoes.

ITALIAN SAUSAGE BAKE

½ lb. Italian sausage, browned and drained

2 medium potatoes, baked in microwave

1 15-oz. can spinach, drained

1 15-oz. can diced tomatoes, drained

1 cup shredded cheese

2 eggs

1 cup milk

Crumble 1 potato in bottom of loaf pan, cover with spinach, tomatoes, sausage, the second crumbled potato and cheese. Combine milk and egg and pour over other contents. Bake at 350 for 50 minutes.

EGG NOODLES WITH MUSHROOM SAUCE

4 oz. egg noodles

6 oz. sausage or ground beef

2 oz. cream cheese

10 oz. cream of mushroom soup

5 oz. milk

½ tsp. pepper

Prepare noodles according to package directions. Brown meat in saucepan, add and mix cream cheese, add other ingredients and simmer 15 minutes. Serve over noodles.

SPAGHETTI WITH TUNA

½ lb. spaghetti

1 6-oz. can tuna

6 green olives, sliced

2 tbsp. minced garlic

5 tbsp. olive oil

Prepare spaghetti in salted water according to package directions. Over medium heat sauté garlic in olive oil, remove garlic, add tuna and olives to garlic flavored oil, heat thoroughly and serve over spaghetti.

MIXED VEGETABLES

1 15-oz. can black beans

1 15-oz. can small kernel white corn

1 10-oz. can tomatoes with green chilies

1 green pepper, finely chopped

1 small onion, finely chopped

1 cup Italian dressing

1 tsp. garlic powder

Drain beans and corn, mix all ingredients, refrigerate before serving.

BEAN SALAD

1 15-oz. can kidney beans

1 chopped onion

2 chopped boiled eggs

4 tbsp. pickle relish

1 tbsp. mayonnaise or salad dressing

dash of both salt and pepper

Mix and refrigerate.

BEANS AND GREENS

1 serving (8 oz.) canned baked beans

1 serving (8 oz.) soul-food type canned greens

1 tsp. vinegar

Heat thoroughly in separate pans, add vinegar to greens at serving.

FRITATTA

1 small onion, diced

2 small potatoes

2 eggs

dash of salt

2 tbsp cooking oil

Over medium heat, cook onion in 1 tbsp. oil until translucent, place on plate to the side. Microwave potatoes for maybe 3 minutes, dice and brown in 1 tbsp oil. When browned, add the onion and salt, stir occasionally. Break the eggs into a cup, stir and break yolks, pour over other contents and cook until eggs are set.

Bacon and eggs: fry bacon in saucepan until done, set on warm plate, fry eggs in bacon grease. Add salt and pepper.

Instant oatmeal: prepare according to package directions.

Biscuits with syrup: prepare purchased frozen biscuits according to package directions, add butter and syrup.

Baked potato with cottage cheese: pierce potato and microwave until done. Split, mash contents slightly, salt, cover with cottage cheese, add pepper and eat.

Sliced tomato with cottage cheese: using garden fresh tomatoes, wash, slice, salt, add peppered cottage cheese. Eat.

Meat sandwiches: warm any type of leftover meat, place on bread slice, add horseradish sauce and another bread slice. Eat.

Grilled cheese sandwich: butter one side each of two pieces of bread, put cheese between the unbuttered sides, place on hot tabletop grill until nicely browned. Eat.

Steamed carrots: peel carrots, divide into smaller portions, place in a cup with just a bit of water, microwave for maybe 4 minutes with a saucer on top of the cup. Add salt and butter. Other vegetables may be fixed the same way or you can use a steamer.

Easy sweet: 7 crushed vanilla wafers, 1 tbsp. each of orange marmalade, seedless red raspberry jam, chocolate syrup, and whipped topping.

Icing: 1 20-oz. can crushed pineapple, 1 cup whipped topping, and 1 3.5-oz. box vanilla pudding mix. Mix thoroughly, refrigerate. Good on un-iced cakes or just eat as pudding.

Cherry pie: 2 purchased pie crusts and 1 20-oz. can cherry pie filling. Bake according to package directions.

Easy fudge: 1 16-oz. can creamy chocolate frosting and 12 oz. chocolate chips. Combine in microwave proof dish, heat on defrost for 3 minutes and mix. Repeat until mixture is creamy. Place wax paper in large flat container, pour fudge on wax paper, refrigerate until it hardens, remove wax paper and cut fudge into squares.

CONTINUE LEARNING

MANAGING MONEY INTRODUCTION

The importance of monitoring your spending habits and developing realistic limitations can hardly be emphasized too strongly. Unfortunately, since this subject is not often taught in the school systems it becomes the responsibility of parents to ensure that their children have an understanding of this most important subject.

Attention to the number of repossessed homes and personal bankruptcies and then the realization that each one represents broken hopes and dreams for those involved illustrates the importance to you of developing a plan for your own situation.

Without your attention to this detail, the likelihood of having many uncomfortable or unmanageable situations throughout your life is greatly increased. In a nutshell, you should carefully determine your income and its inherent limitations before assuming obligations.

The first step in personal financial planning is to get a clear picture of your present situation. Then, a budget forces you to decide what you want most out of life, helps you live within your income, helps eliminate wasteful spending, and helps you adapt to unplanned circumstances.

Evidence that you need to budget is proven if you buy things you don't need, pay one credit card with another, postdate checks, and other money management shortcomings.

Developing the monthly spending reports such as the ones we will discuss is neither as difficult nor as time consuming as you may think. Their importance becomes more and more apparent as they are utilized but only you can cause these reports to be as beneficial as they should be.

To start, select the month you wish to begin and lay out your budget report as follows: draw a line from top to bottom in the middle of a legal-size pad. In the upper left side place the date you are starting, such as "Start January 2011." Immediately below list the categories "Current + Deferred = Total." Under these categories place the proper start-of-the-month amounts.

"Current" includes amounts representing cash on hand, savings and checking account balances, money due from others, and any similar items.

"Deferred" represents self-managed retirement accounts and does not include those accounts that are managed at your place of employment. Bonds, mutual funds, and IRA-type accounts are examples of what could fall into this category.

The remainder of the page is filled out as the month progresses. The second section lists all income received in the report month, the third section lists the month-end totals for the items in this section; the total in this section becomes the amount shown in the "Current" category in the following month. Next you would compute the amount spent within the month and whether it was a plus or minus month.

The last section on the left side of the pad is where the "Deferred" information is recorded. That total would be shown as the start amount for the next month. At the end of the month, the left side of the pad could look something like this:

Start January 2011

Current + Deferred = Total

$1,200.50 + $1,500.00 = $2,700.50

January Net Income

1-10 Job Income $ 1,000.00

1-25 Job Income $ 1,000.00

1-31 Bank Interest $ 1.10

Total $2,001.10

End of Month Current

Cash $135.00

Checking $475.60

Savings $665.00

Total $1,275.60 This becomes your new "Current" amount for the next month. It is $75.10 more than the month start figure so you show + $75.10 here and you subtract $75.10 from your monthly income and that shows the amount you spent in the month: $1,926.00

Since you will show that $50.00 was transferred to "Deferred," the last section of the left-hand side of the pad could look something like the following:

End of Month Deferred

Bonds $500.00

IRA $500.00

Mutual Funds $550.00

Total $1,550.00

This becomes your new "Deferred" amount for the next month.

On the right-side half of the pad you show itemized spending totals. You accumulate from keeping a daily tab of expenditures, your credit card, and your checking account entries. If you do not pay off your credit card every month, you will have to devise a way to track that. Naturally every increase in credit card balance is an additional amount spent.

January Itemization could look something like that shown on the following page. Naturally, in a real life situation some of the items would include the number of cents spent.

600.00	Rent
100.00	Utilities
90.00	Groceries
210.00	Restaurants
200.00	Church
250.00	Car Payment
50.00	Car Repair
75.00	Gasoline
75.00	Insurance Home & Car

50.00	Phone
50.00	Cable
25.00	Clothing
25.00	Home
25.00	Gifts
50.00	Fun
50.00	To "Deferred"

$1,925.00 Total Itemized Expenditures

Your computation on the left-hand side of the pad shows that your expenditures were $1,926.00 so you failed to log $1.00 in expenditures. This is not an uncommon mistake.

Start February 2011

Current + Deferred = Total

$1,275.60 + $1,550.00 = $2,825.60

February Net Income

2-10 Job Income $1,000.00

2-25 Job Income $1,000.00

2-26 Garage Sale $ 135.00

2-31 Bank Interest $ 1.15

Total $2,136.15

End of Month Current

Cash $235.00

Checking $475.60

Savings $765.00

Total $1,475.60 This becomes your new "Current" amount for the next month. + $200.00 Spent $1,936.15

End of Month Deferred

Bonds $500.00

IRA $500.00

Mutual Funds $600.00

Total $1,600.00 This becomes your new "Deferred" amount for the next month.

We will pretend that your February itemized expenditures are exactly the same as they were in January, including the $50.00 transferred to Mutual

Funds. This $1,925.00 total is $11.15 less than the amount you computed as spent on the left side of the pad. So, on the right side of the pad you would show $11.15 as un-itemized expense to make the figures balance.

Repeat this procedure each month.

The above assumes that your health insurance is paid by your employer.

You may wish to log the amounts withheld as taxes so that you can from time to time chastise legislators.

The above infers that the report is for a single person. The same process is used for a couple or a family.

If you are part of a couple and both work you should make every effort to live on one income. It makes it much easier to handle the problems that come when one of you loses your job.

The amount spent for rent or house payment should not exceed thirty percent of your net income. Less is better.

If you are not running a large budget surplus it is rarely a good idea to drive a new car and never should you finance a car for longer than three years.

If you do not plan for your retirement years, who will? It is not often enjoyable to be poor when you are young; it is even less fun if you   are old and poor.

Credit cards can be either a blessing or an absolute curse. It depends on how the cardholder utilizes them. It is a great feeling to pay no credit card interest.

Incurring bank charges for insufficient funds checks has to be considered wasteful at best or really stupid at worst.

Surely this section will be of benefit to some.

LIVING LIFE INTRODUCTION

If there is a God, and if there is a place called Heaven and another called Hell, and if there is a day called Judgment Day for all of humanity then can it not be truly said that a knowledgeable and caring person can not love another without being concerned for their well-being in eternal life?

Millions of people, including this author, believe this to be true. If you are not a believer, then should you not attempt to disprove the belief? This is a very high stakes gamble for you and those you care about. Many of the most fervent believers started by trying this approach.

There is no guarantee that the advice or suggestions given in this section will be useful and accurately describe every one of the situations to be encountered in life but it may well be helpful in more than one situation.

It is arranged more or less haphazardly starting with the early years and continuing through old age and may contain duplicate references to the same subject.

You may want to mark those areas of particular interest to you and perhaps you will wish to prepare tests for your children regarding some of the thoughts presented.

Is it possible that if you whisper to a crying baby it will quiet down in order to hear what you are saying?

Hold and cuddle the baby enough that it will know that it is loved. Not sure at what age you should stop doing this.

It does not hurt a baby to cry some, even when they are in bed.

An adult should be very careful about sleeping with a baby. Sometimes the baby never wakes up.

At a fairly early age, start reading to the baby. Not sure at what age you should stop doing this. As soon as practicable have the child read to you.

Talk to and touch your children often.

Do not over emphasize potty training: it will generally just happen. Some success has been attained by awarding good conduct stickers and when several have been accumulated, buying the child a small toy.

By age two, judicious use of "time outs" will usually help with discipline. A timer should be used and five minutes is generally long enough for the young ones.

It is pleasurable to hear a young one laugh but there should never be excessive tickling.

Usually after age three, start and continue teaching respect for others.

Expect your children to behave properly when in public or when you are entertaining other adults.

When a child is old enough to walk and reach, be very careful about hot things on the stove they can tip over or having items, like paper shredders where they may start them. Window cords can also be dangerous.

Probably by age three a child should be allowed and even encouraged to help with household tasks. This should continue until they are adults.

By age five, a child should have some grasp of table manners. At an early age, seat the child across from the adult so that it may learn by watching.

If the parents are a couple, the children must know that the bond between the couple is at least as strong as is the bond with the child. If not part of a couple, the children must know that the parent has other important interests.

Develop your faith and pass it on to your children. This should continue until they are adults.

Do not enter the most outstanding birthday party competition. The children generally do not care and you will almost certainly need the money later.

The intent of Christmas is not to see how badly you can wreck your budget.

Limit television and playing with hand held electronic games. This should probably continue through the teen years. Encourage reading and talking. Also, many experts consider it to be a mistake for the child to have a TV in their room.

Attempt to have a daily sit-down family meal with no radio or television background noise.

Music lessons are desirable.

Encourage the art of writing when age appropriate.

Help the children picture a positive future.

A modest allowance can be good. It is best when the parent guides its use to include saving, investing, church, charity and mad money.

The years probably up through age twelve are the most important formative years. The child goes through several stages of development and it is important that the parent understand this. Be firm but patient.

The example a parent sets is the most important learning tool for a child. Do not expect yourself or your child to be perfect.

Try not to take sides when your children argue and just because you buy something for one does not mean you need to buy something for the others. Their turn will come. Life is not fair.

Parents will do themselves and their children a favor if they explore the subject of delayed gratification. In this same vein, they should probably hear the words, "we can not afford that" from time to time. It will make it easier when the subject of a new car comes up when the child becomes old enough to drive.

Spanking has not been addressed in this early years section: views differ on this subject. This author thinks that it is called for at times but one should not be angry nor really hurtful.

The teen years are commonly considered to be difficult years for both the child and the parent. Easy and good answers to all differences are probably too much to hope for but if a loving foundation has been made and it is expressed that this love will continue, problems can be lessened.

The expectations that have been previously mentioned do not change nor does the desirability of talking, reading, and helping with household tasks.

Peer pressure can easily become a major problem as the child becomes more and more influenced by those in their group. A parent should be as aware as possible of who is influencing the child, should attempt to know what kind of communication takes place on the phone, the computer, and through text messaging. It is possible that many parents are lax in this area…they will usually meet with opposition.

Before the child reaches adolescence the parent should have already had a short discussion or two regarding the bodily changes that occur at that time.

Discussions regarding sexual activity can also be difficult but it is certainly not fair, particularly to the girls, for them to have no idea of the amount of pressure they will meet to take this step long before they should.

Girls, in particular but not exclusively will hear words such as "if you really cared about me," "everybody does it," "I won't tell a soul," and all sorts of variations of this pressure message.

In response to this pressure, it is wise to have a few answers prepared. "No, if you really cared about me you wouldn't ask me to do something I consider to be wrong," "no, not even close to everybody does it," "perhaps you should also discuss this with my Dad," " if I do and I should become pregnant, how would you handle your responsibility as a parent? I believe your income should not be less than 400 dollars a week," and other comments of this   type.

The child at this age should be aware that they are probably going to live another sixty years or more. Most of those they associate with now will drift out of their lives once high school is over and new friends will enter. Mistakes made now can easily negatively impact all the years to come.

Any expert when discussing family poverty will touch upon how negatively one will almost certainly impact their life if they become pregnant without the benefit of a husband who is mature enough to handle the demands that will be made on him.

Probably now is a good time to address traits present in some of the boys. Some will start bragging immediately after causing the girl to succumb to his wishes…some will lie regardless. Also, some will have no further desire to spend time with the girl they have succeeded with.

Although it is not extremely common, it appears to be a good idea for the boy to also wait until after marriage.

The above just scratches the surface of the subject and does so without even mentioning the long lasting negative effects of sexually transmitted diseases. Perhaps you should secure reliable information in this area also. There is absolutely no completely reliable approach other than abstinence.

Another area which a child will increasingly be exposed to is the use of drugs. There will be pressure to participate and be part of the group but the short term benefits, if any, are nothing in comparison to the probable long term harm that often accompanies drug use. One should not leave a drink on the table if there is any possibility it could have been tampered with before returning.

Experimentation with alcohol use should be viewed as just another aspect of drug use: it is wise to completely avoid this habit forming life wrecker.

While speaking of negative influences that a child will be exposed to, and they can happen at any age, one should not overlook the use of vulgar and obscene language: one can easily be led into this direction and it is a hard habit to break.

"You are responsible for you" becomes a true statement as one ages and the condition, with a few exceptions, lasts until life ends. Naturally, for a time the parent is also responsible for the child.

Excessive e-mailing and text messaging is said to reduce the intelligence on those who are addicted to these activities. It is also said that this intelligence loss is temporary. One should be quite reluctant to reveal personal information.

The approach to money management contained in an earlier section of this book should become familiar to and used by your teen. Also, those who are older.

It is not at all uncommon for a boy friend (sometimes a girl friend, as well) to attempt to become overly controlling in a relationship. They may want to pick your friends, manage your time, select your clothes and any manner of other areas of your life. These people need to be identified and avoided.

Is it worthwhile to wish you were thinner?

"Actions have consequences" is a statement that should be learned early and remembered throughout life.

Studies have shown that television watching or background noise has an adverse effect upon all stages of development and that the effect starts in the early years.

A parent, having once been a teen, should know that co-ed slumber parties are inappropriate for a child you love.

Guard your reputation, expect criticism, do not put too much faith in outward appearance, and admit it when you are at fault or wrong.

Gifts call for a thank you note…not an e-mail.

Some studies indicate that excessive e-mailing and texting has an adverse effect upon the thinking ability.

Cheaters in the classroom are often caught and may pay a stiff penalty.

Giving birth to an unplanned baby often means the opposite of having a stable, loving family situation. Absence of the father very often has a lifetime adverse effect.

Birth control methods are not always reliable.

At no point in their development should a parent fail to guide their children.

At family meal time, consider asking each member to report on what they have done for the family that day.

If you don't teach your children about money, who will?

Providing your children with all their desires may very well cause them to have unrealistic expectations later in life.

Is it possible that having spoiled children of any age may well be an indication of lazy parents?

Most of the advice to this point has been directed toward children through their high school years and the parents of these children. Now, we will attempt to address the college years through old age. Of course there will be overlaps and duplications…forgive them, forgiveness is also a trait worth developing.

The years following high school usually bring another level of personal responsibility for your own actions but much of the advice given to this point is still good advice. Cheating, drug and alcohol use and sex outside of marriage come to mind. It is also at this point that many young ones become addicted to excessive and unnecessary use of credit cards. This often brings a long period of deep regret.

Some say that college orientation starts active brainwashing. Perhaps that is why a high percentage of those who enter college as Christians will not be so at the end of their years in college.

Writing a daily journal can be worthwhile. Write anything from activities to thoughts.

Practice laughing a bit when you are alone. You will feel better. Exercise helps, too.

More radio, less TV when you are alone.

Attempt to pay off your credit card each month. Is there really any good reason to   have multiple credit cards?

College should be chosen on a cost to potential benefit basis. Hesitate to pay top dollar.

If the parent is paying for college, they should set reasonable expectations such as grades, hours carried and goals.

At any age, how important is a new car?

Perhaps the only good reason for attending college is to prepare yourself for your wage earning years. Do not rush into choosing a major, watch your money, follow directions, and take a reasonable class load.

The student and their possessions should be insured.

It seems that practicing Christians, regardless of their earthly condition or lot in life, are with few exceptions, happier than those who take another path.

Most occupations have some imperfections: housewife to CEO share this situation. Regardless, show respect, control anger, and communicate well.

Communicate with and encourage your mate. Develop goals, and, above all, be faithful and expect the same of your mate.

When a child returns to the home of their parents after college or an unsuccessful work effort, it often places new burdens on both the parent and the child. Each should try to understand   the feelings of the other.

In all situations, agree on healthy boundaries.

The brain is probably still developing if you are younger than age 25.

Remember the difference between needs and wants.

In regard to others, two important, though usually unspoken, questions are "can I trust you" and "do you really care about me?"

In most meetings it is good to take notes and focus on the speaker.

If you have a point of view that differs from the one held by God, you are the only one that can change.

Use every available opportunity to spend quality time with your family.

Sometimes a parent should not too eagerly bail a child out of an uncomfortable situation.

Whether your job is in the workforce or as a homemaker, work as hard on your marriage as you do at your job. Never let your job or children interfere with maintaining your marriage.

There is no set in concrete rule as to who should pay for a marriage. If one is mature enough to marry, they should be old enough to pay for the ceremony. Perhaps they should pay half as much as planned, invest the other half and have a yearly celebration on the interest earned.

Debt is a major cause of stress in much of the young and in a high percentage of those who are older.

At an early age, start thinking about how your retirement years will be funded. Start and contribute to a plan.

Unless you have a driving desire to be poor, do not have children until you are married, do not curtail your education, and do not experiment with drugs and alcohol.

The frequency of grandparents raising their grandchildren continues to increase. This is primarily due to unfit parents. Make sure that you and your prospective mate will not do this to your children and your parents.

Be secure enough with yourself to delay sexual activity: there is little evidence of lasting benefit to those who do not follow this advice.

Self analysis: did you do your best? Why not?

Adult children moving back with their parents should help however possible and pay some rent if they can at all.

When job hunting search all avenues for good advice: certainly you should be able to tell why you should be hired.

If you follow current news, you are well aware that there are many people living a life that you would not choose for yourself. Violence, sub standard living conditions, shelters for the abused, children and adults being tortured, there seems to be no end to the worthlessness of mankind. Many of these people going through a personal tragedy were once hopeful, loving, and trusting. They made a mistake.

The example you set for your children will be reflected in their life.

Explain to your child that expecting that they obey is just part of your love.

Never shake a baby: discuss this and other dangers with your pediatrician. If you are old enough to have a baby, you are old enough to ensure that it does not suffer because of your actions.

As the child enters the high school years, the window closes on your influence. Attempt to keep a tradition of meal time together.

Although a parent should usually be supportive, a child should learn that actions (or inactions) have consequences.

Show your children affection, hug them often, particularly in the early years.

Parents are the primary teachers of character traits and religious belief.

For the older child, bedwetting can not always be controlled by the child. This requires understanding and probably advice from a professional.

Don't try to buy their love.

Be honest about death and encourage showing grief.

Children specialize in testing parents and will see how far they are allowed to go.

Be neither too strict or too lenient.

Actions that seemed cute as a young child are not so cute a couple of years later. The child remembers the previous approval.

At an early age provide chores for your children to do. Shortly after age ten they should be doing the household laundry, washing dishes, cleaning house, and beginning to learn how to cook. This could be tied to their allowance.

Both members of a couple need to be involved in your joint financial plan. Both need to know where all accounts are and anything related to finances and insurance.

As a couple, perform a yearly review of every aspect of your financial situation.

Financial mistakes include, no plan, no budget, no will, too much credit card debt, being improperly insured, failing to adequately plan for retirement years. Failing to act is often the biggest mistake of all.

Become healthy before becoming pregnant.

Friends you have had as a couple often drift away when death of divorce strikes. They really do not know what to do with you as a single. Try to remain close and start to enlarge your circle of friends.

It is often more difficult for men than women to adjust to the changes death or divorce bring. Men usually have trouble discussing their feelings and rarely have a well developed support group. Becoming involved with helping others can often be a good approach.

Much too frequently, parental alienation rears its ugly head. This occurs when one (sometimes both) of the parents will actively attempt to turn a child against the other parent. This is almost always severely damaging to the child.

If remarrying after divorce, it is good to review why the divorce took place. You may have faults that need to be corrected. Both of you should be very open about financial matters.

Sometimes renting a home is preferable to buying one. You need to analyze carefully.

Before marriage, identify and resolve possible conflicts in regard to raising children. Agree when and how much you will spend: it usually takes much longer to pay a debt than it does to create it. Be wary of those who are controlling.

Before starting a family agree on disciplining children, who will be primarily responsible for comforting and teaching them? Identify child abuse. How much time are you willing to invest in your children? How will you convey to your spouse that they remain your number one priority?

Whether married or single, both men and women will almost certainly be alone at some point. Be very aware of financial matters. Avoid being old and really poor.

After retirement, a part time job can add meaning to your life.

Time management is important on the job and is equally important in regard to your home life.

Memory loss in a spouse or parent is difficult to handle. It requires more patience than many of us possess.

You usually have the time to do things you want to do if you really want to do them.

If siblings need to be involved in the care of a parent, it is usually necessary that they work on their communication skills.

Long distance elder care and becoming aware of the wishes and financial matters of your parents are not going to be discussed here. You would be wise to investigate these sometimes delicate matters.

Since the notes I've accumulated over a number of years have now been brought to your attention, I can now only apologize for those areas I have not addressed and wish you well in managing your life and the life of those you love.

Lastly, many children choke and die while eating hot dogs and various other things; never throw flour or sugar on a grease fire; and do not throw water on a kitchen oil fire. My reference said you should turn off the heat, dampen a cloth and cover the pan with the cloth.

END OF BOOK 2

WHY NOT RUN FOR PRESIDENT???

By Linden H. Swift

Consulting Editor Sharon Herbitter

Printed by Augustin Printers, Richmond, IN

LINDENWOULD PUBLISHING CO. INC.

BOX 203 PLAINFIELD, IN 46168-0203

CONTENTS

FOREWORD

Harebrained is hardly the word I would choose to describe my decision to run for President of these United States. It is no more so than were my decisions to undertake that most difficult pilgrimage in Spain six years earlier or, following two years of weakened condition, deciding to undertake a mission-related work effort at Haus Edelweiss in Austria. This, too, could very well be a wonderful experience.

Linden Swift, Spring 2012

INTRODUCTION

As mentioned in the foreword, the adventures in Spain and in Austria at ages 75 and 77 respectively, were wonderful experiences for me. Following the truly great surprise party my children, Brian and Julie, provided when I attained age 80, I, thinking my pre-Spain strength would surely return, started planning a worthwhile celebration for two years later. Visiting each of the 32 counties in Ireland seemed to be just what I needed to do.

Months attempting to establish just the right contacts failed to provide exactly what I desired and I realized that I needed to develop a back-up vacation-type plan. A Presidential run was the alternative I deemed to be best.

The following pages, in more or less chronological order, illustrate my actions, the results, and some additional notes. Perhaps you will decide to modify my approach and throw your hat into the ring too.

This book was developed in conjunction with the celebration of my 82nd birthday: it was a really fun project.

THE EARLY MONTHS

I learned my lesson regarding keeping secrets from my children when, as I was recuperating from the effects of my pilgrimage in Spain, I told them that I was considering an effort to climb Mt. Kilimanjaro in Africa and they each just threw a fit! Julie strongly hinted that she would have me committed to a mental institution.

So it was about the middle of April 2011 when I contacted them, saying that my Ireland trip plan was not developing and that I would instead attempt a run for the presidency. They took it very well! I told them that the filing fee was $1,000 and that the entire effort should cost less than five times that amount.

Brian was pleased and a bit excited about the possibility saying, "You can't take it with ya." I answered Julie's "Why?" question by saying "I don't know, no reason…I just haven't had a real vacation in a long time and my visiting Ireland plan is not developing well, so why not?" She, then, agreed with Brian. She was not, however, interested in being my campaign manager.

I was slow to mention this project to others so it took until roughly the end of summer to inform some closer friends: Joyce Brinkman and Kent McPhail were political allies over the years, Sam Friedman is a long-term friend: he and I are the only surviving members of what was a four-member work-associated birthday club.

We changed the name to "The Dissolution Committee" and we've spent thirty years trying to wind up the birthday club affairs.

Sharon Herbitter, now living in Alabama, is an outspoken friend...I first met her while my family was vacationing in Florida. She is not much older than my young children. Jack Burlison, Bill Furman, Paul Gunning, Chuck Kiefer and I meet for breakfast and discussion on Thursdays. They agreed to be my Advisory Board. Brian's daughter Alison, a high school sophomore, agreed to serve as my Press Secretary. Lisa, the daughter of my deceased lady friend, Rubye, was very supportive. She and her husband, Peter, planned to meet me in New Hampshire...they now live in Maine. Lastly, Laura Herzog, a supportive friend of many years standing, rounds out this list. My apologies to those that I neglected to include here.

In early July I investigated the possibility of forming an Exploratory Committee and the necessity of the Federal Election Commission being involved...I learned that if I made no attempt to raise funds they need not be involved. So that is the route I took.

Laura approved a campaign-related change that I would make to my blog postings when the announcement time came and I corresponded with Lisa about securing a map of Manchester, NH. Toward the end of the month both Brian and Julie visited with me, and, as you may imagine, we did talk a bit about my current interest.

In early August I watched a video clip of an Al Sharpton televised monologue. It was so very bad, painful to watch.

By this time, I had viewed many poll results and reports of previous elections. I remembered that Sharpton's New Hampshire vote total in a run for the presidency he made in 2004 was 362 votes. Surely 363 votes should become a secondary objective for me…if I did not become President, I could be considered for a TV show!

Because I had decided to depend on public transportation if I made it to New Hampshire, I decided that Manchester was where I needed to stay because bus transport to Concord and Nashua is available there and it is the largest city in that state. On August 22 I received a good map of the area that I had ordered.

At this time I explained to Sam that I would not be involved in Iowa…I would devote all my efforts to New Hampshire. Each state seems to have its own filing requirements and most would be impossible on my limited budget. Besides being one of the easiest to get on the ballot, New Hampshire is the second state to hold a contest. It was the best choice.

Having learned that there were no federal requirements if I did not accept donations, would spend less than $5,000, and have no campaign committee, I then contacted the office of the New Hampshire Secretary of State and received a very nice note back from Karen Ladd. I called her and was told that there was no need for me to appoint delegates if I thought that I would receive less than 10% of the vote. I said that God would have to intervene for me to get such a vote total.

A long phone conversation with Brian brought August political activity to a close. We covered every possible aspect of my Presidential campaign…most were far-fetched and foolish. It was easy to see that he got as much fun out of thinking about the endeavor as I did.

Not a great deal was accomplished in September. Naturally, there were many conversations, mostly with Brian, Lisa, and Sam. Toward the end of the month was the time I chose to ask my Thursday morning breakfast group about serving as my Advisory Board. Jack suggested that I use "Ride the Dark Horse to Victory" as a campaign slogan. It does have a nice ring to it. On the last day of the month I learned that the New Hampshire primary filing dates would be October 17 to October 28.

A portion of the October 4 note I sent to Brian is as follows: "In 13 days the filing for President in New Hampshire begins, ending 11 days later. At this point, I intend to file. If I do, my goal will be to finish at the top of the pack following the first tier of 5 candidates and, secondarily, to top the vote total of, I believe, 362 votes received by Al Sharpton in his 2004 effort." Brian was pleased with the note.

On October 7 Karen Ladd responded to my request for filing forms for the New Hampshire Presidential Primary.

On October 10 I sent the following note to Julie and Brian: "Of course I'm aware that it is over two months until

Christmas but my current campaign considerations force me to look to the future. Due to the difficulty New Hampshire is having in selecting a primary election date, my schedule around the first of the next year has to be uncertain.

"There is thought that the primary may fall around my birthday on the 4th. That should work for me...if it is closer to Christmas, it is doubtful that I would want to be away from Plainfield. Being willing to serve the public politically can just tear one apart." Julie (the word may be "succinctly") said, "You are goofy." Brian just said that "There is a magical ring to the words 'Former Presidential Candidate Linden Swift.'" This illustrates why he might receive the lion's share of any estate I may leave.

On October 21 I mailed my filing papers to New Hampshire and one day later sent the following note to Brian and Julie:

"I fully realize that my efforts to make and save for you over the years have not been wildly successful. But, thanks to not purchasing cable television for the past five years, I have been able to scrape together the necessary $1,008.59 required to date to file for the office of President of these United States in New Hampshire. The filing form and the required check were mailed yesterday.

"From your standpoint, you may prefer to consider this as another investment effort. Just think, if I am able to surpass the 362-vote total achieved by 'Rev.' Al Sharpton in an

earlier election, it is possible that I will also be made host of a well paid television show. We are talking about real money now! I do have two other election goals but they fade into insignificance compared to that mentioned above. So, bite your tongues and wish me well."

Brian informed that he thought that my investment plan was solid and that he and Sheri have a similar plan that involves hitting the lottery. "A couple of additional thoughts for you to consider…it is always a good idea to diversify.

"Video Conferencing Fees: Former President Clinton earns $125,000 fee for remarks to business groups delivered via video conference. You wouldn't need to leave your house.

"Reality TV Show: Keeping Up with the Swifts, The Real Former Presidential Candidate of Indiana, or I Love Linden are some possible series names. Current reality TV star Kim Kardashian makes over $10,000 per tweet. When she tweets three times in a day, she rakes in just under the average annual U.S. salary of $31,410. As if that's not enough, Kim even makes her friends pay to be in her presence. She charged guests between $1,000 and $2,500 to attend her birthday party on October 22, 2010. She rakes in $40,000 per episode of her show. On the downside, however, she wasn't popular until she released a sex tape." Not sure I want to go there.

"Dancing With the Stars: The Stars get paid $125,000 for the first two episodes and then $20,000 for each week thereafter. They also get an addition $50,000 bonus if they make it to week nine of the competition.

So it works out to a maximum of $245,000 after it is all said and done. Hope this helps."

Julie, as usual, was somewhat more brief: "I don't think I can improve on Brian's note."

At this point we should review my efforts to date: I have selected a Press Secretary, my wildly enthusiastic Advisory Board is well prepared, filing has been accomplished, plans, although not yet acted upon, are in place for me to spend the days following my 82nd birthday in New Hampshire happily greeting potential voters. We are ready!

On October 26, Shira Schoenberg, a very pleasant reporter for The Boston Globe who was in the process of contacting "fringe candidates," conducted a rather long interview with me. Only the following quote appeared in her October 28 article:

"I wanted something out of the ordinary to do this winter," said Linden Swift, an 81-year-old retiree from Indiana who failed in his effort to plan a vacation to Ireland. "It seemed like running for president was a good second choice."

To say that I was pleased to get this mention would be a major understatement. It was repeated in several papers and blogs. Brian said the mention alone was worth the filing fee and Sam then said that it had to be a Linden quote: a reporter wouldn't think of that.

On November 2 I received another campaign-related call, this time from Jason McLure, a reporter for Reuters. The results of this call also appeared in several media outlets and, once again, I was pleased. It read like this:

"Linden Swift, a retired data processor from Indiana whose most recent self-published book was titled 'God is Wrath,' chose to spend $1,000 to be on the ballot rather than take a trip to Ireland to celebrate his 82nd birthday.

"'It would appear to be a dumb waste,' he said. 'On the other hand, how many children will be able to say "my dad was a former presidential candidate"? I ought to leave them

something since I'm not going to leave them a lot of money.'"

(It is quite possible that I slurred the book title. It should read: "GOD IS ALSO WRATH." The purpose was to call attention to the fact that God is more than love.)

By November 3 I knew that primary election day in New Hampshire was set for January 10. At this time I expected to be listed near the end of the ballot. On this date, Tyler Leland recorded a seven-minute video of my presidential announcement for YouTube access. The subjects addressed included these:

As probably the oldest candidate and almost certainly under-funded, a realistic goal is to finish as close to the first tier candidates as possible. A secondary goal would be to secure 363 votes since Al Sharpton received 362 votes in an earlier election; maybe I, like him, would end up with a TV show. If two miracles should occur and I emerge as the nominee of my Republican party, I would consider Herman Cain as my running mate…After all, President Obama is said to have secured as many as ten million votes based only on his race—surely Mr. Cain would bring two times that many to us since he is twice as black as Obama.

I covered my work history starting with a paper route at age twelve until joining the Air Force for a four-year stint nine years later. Then, on to almost 21 years with the Indiana State Police working in the communications and data processing areas…I wrote the first operating manual for the statewide law enforcement system. It, with modifications, is still in use. The Departments of Welfare and of Corrections then accounted for roughly another 20 years of my career.

Politically, I served over 20 years as a Republican Precinct Committeeman, served one term on the Hendricks County Council, and was active in several other areas. Memberships included The Plainfield Christian Church, Scottish Rite, and Masonic and Elks Lodges. Naturally, at my age I have been involved in many areas that received no mention.

My intentions, if elected to serve, would include balancing the budget and paying down debt; to terminate the over-30 Czars who are now on the payroll; being unmarried, there would be no need for the over-20 aides desperately needed by Mrs. Obama; I would properly address immigration and would increase oil production, and other thoughts would be presented frequently on my blog which you may find at www.linden-would.blogspot.com. As you may have noticed, millions of dollars per year would be saved in White House operation alone.

Tyler's YouTube posting amassed several hundred views and only two comments. The first comment accused me of beings a racist and added that nobody is going to vote for a President who is a racist. My thoughts are that this writer is confusing racism with mathematics and that a racist President was elected in 2008. The second comment referred to me as a realist.

On November 7 my blog entry was entitled Presidential Campaign Day 1. This continued until after the January 10 election. This writing will refer to the entries for each campaign day and intermix other items of potential interest.

Blog 11-7 "Being frugal, rarely vacationing, and not subscribing to cable television allowed Linden Swift to accumulate funds for a special 82nd birthday event in early January 2012. The New Hampshire Presidential primary election was selected. Winning is the primary goal. Being underfunded and probably the oldest candidate means that it would take a miracle to achieve this goal. Republican National Convention selection would require a second miracle. Therefore, a secondary goal is to exceed the 362 votes Al Sharpton amassed in a previous election. This could result in Linden being awarded his own TV show."

This first entry supplies basic campaign information.

Blog 11-7 "Read 1 Corinthians 9:24."

This came from a Bible study; I thought it worth repeating.

Blog 11-7 "Consider Herman Cain for VP: a man with uncommon ability. Being twice as black as the President, he should receive twice as many racist-motivated votes."

Blog 11-7 "Campaign donations will not be solicited or accepted until after the Republican Convention."

Blog 11-7 "Following completion of my term(s) I will have my Presidential pension reduced 10% per year until it reaches the level of workforce (non governmental) average pay."

Blog 11-7 "ALL OF HIS CAMPAIGN COSTS ARE PAID BY LINDEN SWIFT."

Blog 11-8 "Consider Sarah Palin for VP: a woman with uncommon knowledge and ability. Even knows where Naknek, Alaska is located."

(In my long-ago Air Force years, I spent some time in the Naknek vicinity.)

Blog 11-8 "Feel free to match this distribution by Sharon Herbitter of Alabama:

"Today I'm so thankful for my dear friend Linden Swift. He has decided not to let a lack of funds, zero name recognition, or the fact that he'll turn 82 in two months keep him from seeking the New Hampshire Republican presidential nomination. Linden accomplishes twice as much in a day as most folks in their twenties do. He recently recorded his first cd, created a board game (to help homeschoolers learn about finances), and he writes a new book every time I turn around! He delights and inspires me. Wish I could vote for you, Linden!"

Blog 11-9 "Foreign policy will be set after reviewing recent successes. WAIT!…There are none!!! Now what?"

Blog 11-10 "If interns are allowed in my White House, they will not be allowed under my Presidential desk." Of course this item was written with President Clinton in mind.

Blog 11-11 "Linden will never refer to the Marine Corps as Marine Corpse." This referred to a well publicized blunder by our "well spoken" President.

Blog 11-14 "If it is true that three former Fannie Mae executives and now President Obama helpers received almost 300 million dollars in bonuses, Linden, if elected, will attempt prosecution of them and others."

Blog 11-15 "Linden plans to not authorize a Linden Swift Presidential Library at any time." Perhaps a room in the library in Plainfield, Indiana would be considered.

Blog 11-16 "My YouTube Presidential Announcement video has the added comment, 'you are such a racist.' I thought I was just presenting simple mathematics." This comment was regarded by me as being both ill-informed as well as funny.

Blog 11-17 "If elected, my Press Secretary will start press briefings by questioning the press about lack of coverage of important stories." This posting reflected my belief that the press is either biased or inept (or both) in their attempts to adequately cover White House briefings.

Blog 11-18 "GOOD NEWS!!! I was just informed that my name will appear second on the New Hampshire ballot.

This means that every uncommitted voter there should see my name. Maybe we will secure the hoped for 363 votes." I had expected to be near the bottom of the ballot!

Later, when viewing the New Hampshire ballot, I noted that the list of 30 names was more than I expected. Probably 10 or 12 had received nationwide mention and the rest of us were, at best, relatively unknown.

At this time I received a note that led to a fun experience: "My name is Jennifer Maxham, a student at St. Michael's College in Colchester, VT, and I am working on a project with a classmate for our Media and American Politics class. Lizzie and I have selected you to profile as a presidential candidate for the 2012 election. We were hoping that we could contact you and conduct a short interview to learn more about you and your presidential platform.

"Would you be willing to do a phone or skype interview with us tomorrow or Sunday? Anytime after 11:00am tomorrow would be convenient for us or before 1:00pm on Sunday. Hopefully these times are also convenient for you.

"Please respond to confirm what time and method is best for you if you would like to talk to us. Thank you for your time,

"Jennifer Maxham and Lizzie Mortimer"

My response: "I would be pleased to visit with you...I should be available between 11:00 and 1:00 on Friday and 11:30 to 1:00 on Sunday. My phone number is 317-839-6041.

"Not knowing exactly how you became aware of me, I would suggest you review my blog at www.linden-would.blogspot.com and YouTube Presidential announcement video. My Facebook and Twitter postings are just a mention of my blog contents.

"I hope I may be beneficial to your studies and I would appreciate receiving a copy of your finished work if you pursue this effort. I wish you the very best."

This exchange led to several contacts by both telephone and the Internet. Questions touched upon my early life, parents, growing up, family background, education, Air Force, my work life and, of course, matters relating to the presidency if I should be selected for that office. Following are only a few of my responses.

"By 'appointments' I meant positions such as Attorney General, Sec'y of State, Treasury, etc. I was born in Mansfield, Illinois 1-4-30, moved to the area of our old family farm, then owned by an uncle, in what could have been described at that time as an extension of Appalachia in southern Indiana. Since we, a large family, were poverty stricken, we moved within Indiana fairly often until I was in the fourth grade. At that time we moved in with my uncle on the farm. I was there through the seventh grade. Attended a one room school that taught all eight grades. For the eighth grade I lived with a sister and her family in Farmer City, Illinois then to Indianapolis where I lived with my dad through high school.

"My parents split up when I was probably six years old and we stayed with Dad. My mother worked at various jobs...sometimes as a healthcare helper, I believe. She died when I was 19.

"My dad lost his Illinois farming operation in the depression of roughly 1930-41. He was often sick for extended periods of time. He attempted to work on farms until I went to Illinois. Then he secured employment in Indianapolis as a night maintenance supervisor at a department store. I worked for him my last two years of high school...that may have contributed to my grades sliding from honor roll to really pitiful. After my Air Force discharge in 1955 I attended college sporadically at Indiana Central College and, later, at IUPUI. I probably accumulated enough hours to qualify for an associate degree, but, since I was usually well satisfied with my work life, I developed interests other than pursuing my education.

"I have really enjoyed interacting with you and Lizzie...wish me luck in surpassing the Al Sharpton-total of 362 votes in an earlier election. Don't hesitate to contact me again.

"Although there are few efforts that are more important than the protection of our country, the related spending would be studied and, I'm sure, reduced. I have not made a study of the number of generals and admirals in relation to that of previous times of trial but I suspect we are overstaffed at these levels. So, spending would probably be reduced but by what percentage would require study by any public servant.

"What I've written to this point addresses reducing expenditures in several areas but probably not to the point where it would allow for starting to repay the national debt.

"To do that, expenditures would have to be reduced by about 40% from the current levels.

"I am not much in favor of raising taxes on any individual. The wealthy are paying a significant percentage of the taxes that are now collected. If regulations that place a burden on those that create jobs were discontinued, there would be more jobs and more taxpayers and a better situation for the country.

"Your question regarding 'what regulations' is an excellent question for which there will be presently no easy answer. There is no telling the extent of the damage an anti-business regime may cause through regulations between now and the end of 2012. Although there have been countless articles written which have referenced harmful regulations, I have kept none of them nor have I investigated their veracity. What comes to mind is, and it is not really due to a regulation, the closure of U.S. plants which were manufacturing incandescent light bulbs. I hope this provides you with a mindset if not a simple answer.

"What I would do if I should emerge from the Republican National Convention as the nominee is to enlist the assistance of the Chambers of Commerce in contacting businesses, particularly those that had experienced

workforce reduction, and asking them to identify those items which would assist them in resuming hiring. These would be compiled and evaluated."

Blog 11-21 "If elected, Linden will attempt to reduce U.S. contributions to the U.N. to little more than one half of one percent of the total cost…call that fairness."

Blog 11-22 "If elected, Linden will not be issuing dietary advice from the White House." This seemed like a good time to poke a little fun at the present occupants.

"Dear Media Professional,

"As an Ohio high school sophomore, I am pleased to serve as Press Secretary for the New Hampshire Presidential campaign effort of Indiana's Linden Swift. We expect the five top tier candidates to receive about 98% of the votes cast. Due to our lack of name recognition, we will be very pleased to finish 6th. This will allow us to achieve our two lesser goals of surpassing the vote total of 362 votes for Al Sharpton in a previous election (this should result in a TV or radio show for Linden) and to exceed the vote total of the 21st place finisher in the 2008 New Hampshire Republican primary. You can find Linden's songs and poetry will follow on YouTube, his occasional entries on Facebook and Twitter, and his campaign commentary at www.linden-would.blogspot.com.

"Respectfully yours,

"Kate Alison"

The preceding was sent to over 30 New Hampshire-area media outlets by my Press Secretary and granddaughter, Alison. She continued to use the nom de plume "Kate Alison" in all of her press releases.

Blog 11-23 "If elected, Linden plans to fully discourage baseline budgeting." If you don't know what baseline budgeting is, you should.

Blog 11-25 "If elected, Linden plans to fully discourage actions such as favored stock market trading."

Blog 11-28 "After quickly viewing the New Hampshire list of 14 democrat Presidential candidates, including our current President, if forced to pick from that list, Linden would choose Vermin Supreme." It just seemed to me that the name aptly described the functioning party.

Blog 11-29 "Christian action: Linden fully forgives those on the Editorial Board of the Manchester, NH Union Leader for endorsing a Presidential candidate other than Linden."

Blog 11-30 "GREAT NEWS!!! Barney Frank will leave Congress. Bad result: taxpayer-funded pension."

Blog 12-1 "If elected, Linden will work to change or perhaps abolish the National Labor Relations Board."

Blog 12-2 "If elected, Linden, as opposed to our current President, will not condone the expenditure of taxpayer funds to purchase books he has written." I had read that the State Department had authorized the expenditure of around $70,000 of taxpayer funds to purchase books supposedly written by our President. Sickening!!

By this time I had decided that Manchester was the only logical place for me to stay when I would go to perform person-to-person campaigning in New Hampshire. It has bus service to Concord and Nashua, a veterans hospital, and a large population base. I had contacted a local church and the Chamber of Commerce. It was a real campaign setback when I contacted both of the downtown motels and a bed and breakfast and was told that there would be no vacancies during the time I had planned to be there. I contacted some of my supporters, as follows:

"From Jan. 5-11 I wanted to stay in a downtown motel/hotel Manchester, NH. Today I called the two I had in mind and they were both booked full. Then I called a B & B: same story. Then, thinking there may be space available on an acceptable bus tour around the state where they would take care of booking the sleeping arrangements, no luck. Not being willing to drive is a killer for me, I fear. I hate to change my travel hopes but it may be necessary...guess all other attempts to contact uncommitted voters will have to be stepped up. Good ideas will be considered."

I received several comments and suggestions. My favorites were: Sam suggested that I check "Occupy Manchester," Sheri said, "You are NOT driving in Manchester," Brian said, "I hate to say I told you so, but I told you so" and "You have no business walking on snowy streets."

Blog 12-5 "Linden will continue to consider Herman Cain as his running mate: Linden believes the accusations made against Herman are without merit."

After suffering through a campaign setback two days ago it was wonderful to receive a letter from the New Hampshire Coalition for Community Media offering each candidate the opportunity to be shown multiple times on TV just prior to the primary election. They needed a DVD, not longer than three minutes, which would contain the campaign message. They estimated that the DVD would be shown in over 400,000 homes. Needless to say, I quickly asked Tyler if he would once again do me a favor and produce the DVD. This was much better than attempting to meet a relatively few people in a face-to-face situation.

Blog 12-6 "Linden's analysis: Obama was half right: change came…hope is gone!"

Blog 12-7 "If elected, Linden will change the Bureau of Labor Statistics."

Blog 12-8 "Unlike our current President, Linden will never say that it is great to be in Texas while in Kansas." This called attention to just one of the speaking mistakes the President frequently makes.

Blog 12-9 "If elected, Linden's administration will not supply firearms to the Mexican drug cartel." This posting called attention to an administration scandal.

Blog 12-12 "If elected, valid copies of Linden's birth certificate will be widely available." This posting was just to call attention to the present White House occupant.

Blog 12-13 "If elected, Linden will make his educational grades available." As above.

At this point, Tyler produced another DVD for me, this one to be shown on public-access TV in New Hampshire and to be no longer than three minutes. Subjects covered were: my work history, Christian belief, family, political involvement, and that I had hoped to spend time in Manchester but that "there was no room at the inns."

Also, strong defense must be a priority, solicit assistance of the Chambers of Commerce to aid job creation, my White House to be a house of service, not a place to pamper the occupants, expensive parties, vacations, and air travel would be greatly reduced, the Czars and large personal staff would be gone, we would become the greatest oil-producing nation in the world, and a few more items which further the mood for moderation in my White house.

After a few blips such as me misplacing the letter, Tyler getting sick, and the DVD being delayed in delivery, it did arrive in time to be used. The producer, Bob Longabaugh, commented on my "no room at the inns" reference. It was a happy relief to have this project completed.

Blog 12-14 "If elected, Linden will join in prosecuting administration tax cheats."

Blog 12-15 "If elected, Linden, as opposed to the current occupant, will not rest his feet on White House furniture."

Blog 12-16 "If elected, Linden, as opposed to our current President, will sincerely honor those who have, are, or will serve in the military."

Over the period of a few days I had several exchanges with Darren Garnick, a correspondent with The Guardian. I believe that as a "fringe candidate" he made reference to me in a publication on December 19. I never saw it, so it may be that my belief is incorrect.

Blog 12-19 "If elected, Linden will support requiring voter ID laws."

Blog 12-20 "If not elected in New Hampshire, Linden will not run as a third-party candidate. Further, he believes that anyone who votes for a third-party candidate is effectively backing the current inept regime."

Blog 12-21 "GOOD NEWS!!! It appears that my second campaign video will appear on New Hampshire Public Access Cable TV many times in early January."

Blog 12-22 "If elected, I, as was true of President Bush, will stay in the White House at Christmas so that the holiday will be better for the security details."

Blog 12-23 "If elected, Linden will never (as opposed to our current President) refer to reducing Social Security funding as a 'tax cut.'"

Blog 12-26 "If elected, Linden (as opposed to our current President) will view the day after Christmas as just another work day in the White House."

"Linden Swift: Bringing Conservative Values Back to Washington" was the title that Jenn Maxham and Lizzie Mortimer chose for their portion of the Internet posting of their college class, "Profiles of the 2012 U.S. Presidential Candidates."

Their report included personal information, experience in the workforce, hobbies and passions, economic policy, regulation reform, pro-life attitude, reform and dissolution of governmental agencies, military and foreign policy, and other comments. They mentioned that I had been cited in at least 25 newspaper articles, quoted favorable comments made by Jack Burlison and Kent McPhail, and quoted me as saying, "I look at this, running for President, as an opportunity to serve my country, much like my service in the Air Force."

I was mildly amused by the comments of two professors: my low opinion of the Environmental Protection Agency is apparently not shared by the biology professor and the economics professor opined,

"His plan makes sense on the surface, but the devil is in the details." That is true.

I was pleased with the results of the effort made by Jenn and Lizzie and hope that they received a good grade. They said a few words about publications and I would like to add that I was particularly pleased with a short article by Annmarie Timmins which was in the Concord Monitor on December 14.

Blog 12-27 "If elected, Linden, (as opposed to our current leader) will not intimate that he is the fourth-best President."

Dixville Notch and Hart's Location each hold their primary election at just after midnight on election day morning. The results then make the early morning news. Thinking that it would be nice if I was mentioned at that time, I invested $25.00 in a Hart's Location checklist, sent 19 letters there and one to Dixville Notch, as follows:

"It is not unusual for letters from a President or possibly even a presidential candidate to become quite valuable. This is almost certainly not one of those letters.

"This is a self-serving letter that is written with the hope that I will receive at least one vote from Hart's Location and not less than 363 votes in your state. As a 'lesser known' candidate for the Presidency, I have been so very favorably impressed with my interactions by phone and E-mail with many of your fellow citizens.

"I have been assured that there will be multiple showings of my message on New Hampshire Public Access Television. My blog has many campaign-related entries…you may view it at www.linden-would.blogspot.com and you can find my Presidential Announcement as well as some of my songs at YouTube.com Also, you can find some of the books I've written by checking 'books for sale' at http://www.augustinservices.com/."

"I wish you the very best and I pray that our country will return to its once-respected position."

The above is a copy of that which was sent to Hart's Location. The one to Dixville Notch was almost the same. I was to learn almost two weeks later that this investment of campaign funds in roughly the amount of $34.20 was a complete waste…I received not a single vote in either place.

Blog 12-28 "If elected, Linden (as opposed to our current leader) will not spend significant hours on the golf course."

Blog 12-29 "If elected, Linden (as opposed to our current leader) will not permit military uniforms to accept non-military headgear."

"The New Hampshire Presidential Primary Election is January 10. Consider copying, pasting and resending (not forwarding) this chain E-mail message to some of your non-business contacts. The more the merrier…you never know when a friend of a friend may know an uncommitted voter in New Hampshire. Linden Swift's Presidential Campaign Announcement is on YouTube. Just go to YouTube.com and search on Linden Swift…his daily commentary address is www.linden-would.blogspot.com and Public Access TV in New Hampshire should show his DVD multiple times between January 1 and January 9. Thank you for any positive impact you may make on Linden's campaign…we want not less than 363 votes for him."

The above is a copy of a message I sent to probably 40 people. Cheryl Pithoud was probably the champion at resending the message…she said she sent it 79 times and maybe would find a few more to send it to later. I have the very best friends.

Blog 12-30 "If elected, Linden (as opposed to our current leader) will not utter the words, 'job-killing tax cuts.'"

"Plainfield, Indiana, January 2, 2012 – Indiana author-composer, state police retiree and current New Hampshire presidential candidate Linden Swift is more than a little irritated with the waste of thousands of dollars of taxpayer money by our State Department on books supposedly written by President Obama.

"As an indication of his irritation, Swift recently directed his book distributor, Augustin Printing of Richmond, Indiana to send his lowest priced book, *Mind Over Fatter,* to the State Department address in Washington, D.C.. Swift further directed that this comment should accompany the book: 'PLEASE PLACE THIS WITH THE BARACK OBAMA BOOKS YOU PURCHASED USING THOUSANDS OF TAXPAYER DOLLARS. CONSIDER THIS A PROTEST OF GOVERNMENT WASTE.'

"Although normally mild mannered, Linden Swift strongly resents the waste of a single taxpayer dollar. Feel free to join his protest."

The above press release may never have seen the light of day within the media. I never saw evidence that it was used.

Blog 1-2 "Unlike our current leader, Linden will not say 'here in Asia' while being in Hawaii."

Blog 1-3 "If elected, Linden will not be the second President to attempt to force citizens to buy something like Obamacare."

Blog 1-4 "Linden (as opposed to our current leader) would never sit in the same church for years while the pastor spewed hate."

Blog 1-5 "If elected, Linden (as opposed to our current leader) would never appear to support the Muslim Brotherhood and abandon Israel."

Blog 1-6 "If elected, Linden (as opposed to our current leader) will not make "recess appointments" when Congress is not in recess."

At this point, the VFW of New Hampshire contacted me in regard to presenting my campaign information to potential voters. They then copied my Presidential Announcement and carried it on their web site.

Blog 1-7 "Linden's Logic: taxpayers are likely to pay much less in total Presidential retirement pensions to one who is elected at age 82 than to one who is much younger."

Blog 1-9 "If elected, Linden will attempt to sell Camp David and apply the proceeds to the national debt." This now being the day before the January 10 election in New Hampshire, I decided to call a halt to blogging for one week. I imagined how I would have campaigned if I had been able to be there in person. On the preceding Thursday I would have arrived in Manchester, passed out information bearing bookmarks and checked into the motel. On Friday I would go to the Manchester VA Hospital and attempt to sway some veterans in my direction, Saturday I would visit Nashua for more bookmark passing and Sunday would be devoted to church services and resting at the motel. Monday, I would visit Concord and attempt to see Karen Ladd at the office of the Secretary of State. The weather was good on all these days so I would have few concerns about falling. I'd be at the polls on Tuesday and the next day I would fly home. Our imagination can be a wonderful thing!

WINDING DOWN

Election day I arose early and checked for the vote totals for the midnight voting at Dixville Notch and Hart's Location. I was mildly disappointed to learn that I had received not a single vote. So the $9.20 postage cost and the $25.00 spent to secure a Hart's Location checklist was a total waste! I went back to bed for a short time.

Over the course of my relatively short campaign I received probably at least twenty invitations to attend events in New Hampshire or to respond to position polls. Surprisingly, a few of these came after it was too late for the information to be available at the time of the Iowa Caucus which was one week prior to the New Hampshire primary. I attempted to respond to these contacts.

I had made almost no attempt to secure publicity in Indiana: that may have been a mistake. Maybe not! I believe that The Danville Republican was the only Indiana newspaper to mention my candidacy prior to election day. Of course, there was no known radio or TV mention in Indiana of my modest effort.

Mid-morning on election day two reporters from Fox 59 News in Indianapolis came to my home for an interview. They had asked me to have a friend there also. So, Kent McPhail joined us. The two from

WXIN-TV, a young man and a young lady, were very nice appearing and were very pleasant. It was fun talking to them. The questions asked were similar to those previously addressed herein.

Of course my hope to exceed the vote total secured by Al Sharpton in a previous contest was mentioned as was my great disappointment with our current President. Pictures of some of the books I have written were shown as was the CD I had recorded at Lisa and Peter's in Maine. A view of the horse race poster "SWIFT TEMPER" hanging on my wall was also shown: Julie got it for me as a Christmas gift probably two years ago. The recording ended with Kent saying, "That is Linden…I did get a chuckle out of it but I also know he is very serious about his political views."

I never dreamed that this interview would get widespread coverage…I never mentioned it, but Brian saw it that night, before I did, while he was on a business trip to North Carolina, and Lisa saw it in Maine the next morning. I also received many comments from locals who had viewed it. I guess it was a mistake to not obtain local coverage earlier.

Following the TV interview, two radio stations and possibly two or three newspapers also contacted me for an interview. Although it was okay, it was too late to have anything to do with the campaign.

Over the course of the campaign the comments had always been supportive…with at least three notable exceptions. The first, which was appended to my Presidential Announcement video said, "You are such a racist. Nobody is going to vote for a president who is racist." Apparently this person is unaware of the current White House occupant.

The second adverse comment was added to an Internet link to the election day TV interview: "This man is in my opinion in stage 3 alshimers and sould mind his own business and make sure that he gets the proper size depends because he sounds like a polition and all polititions are like diapers, they sould be changed often for the same reason and that is they get full of S@!# !!! and lots of HOT AIR"

These two comments, probably written by English-major Obama supporters, brought a smile to my face. Each of the two were joined by comments more supportive in nature. The third comment, which I think is the funniest, was sent by mail to my church and to my attention: must be a person that knows me, but not very well. "You are an idiot. You spent $1000 to stroke your ego. But I guess it worked since you got your name in the paper and you were on TV. But think how much good would have been done with that money if you had put it in the bucket." NOTE… we have a benevolence ministry within our church   called "the bucket."

Blog 1-16 "Linden will now suspend his campaign until the Republican National Convention."

This campaign was undertaken as a vacation replacement and it resulted in more enjoyment for me than most of the vacations I have ever taken. So, I find very apt the words, "WHY NOT RUN FOR PRESIDENT???"

In closing, costs were $1,000.00 for the filing fee, $25.00 for the Hart's Location voter checklist, $12.49 postage costs, $5.30 for a map of Manchester, and $5.00 certified check fee. This allowed for me to finish 24th out of the 30 who were running in this Republican primary. I received only 18 votes.

Please be aware that filing requirements vary on a state-by-state basis. Some are much more expensive than I found New Hampshire to be and some also require a show of some support from voters within the State.

GO FOR IT!!!

LINDEN'S BOOKS

Much of Linden's life, particularly those years following complete retirement, has been involved with writing and publishing. Much less time was devoted to composing music. In a 30 year span he wrote and/or published 11 books and one music CD utilizing Lindenwould Publishing Co, INC. Now he is strongly considering restricting his efforts to utilizing the services of amazon.com and createspace.com and you may inquire on his name there to check on his progress. To date, both E-books and print copies are available there.

Linden Swift, May 2014

www.ingramcontent.com/pod-product-compliance
Lightning Source LLC
Chambersburg PA
CBHW060246290526
45789CB00001B/221

*9 7 8 1 4 9 9 6 6 4 6 3 8 *